BULLETPROOF

What If Everything That Bugged You, Blocked You, or Brought You Down...
Didn't?

#1 International Bestselling Author

DR. STEVE TAUBMAN

Foreword by the creator and a founder of the Make-A-Wish Foundation, Frank Shankwitz

POWERTRACK
PUBLICATIONS

For ordering information or special discounts for bulk purchases, please contact
Powertrack Publications, 47 Northshore Dr, Burlington, VT 05408.
(802)-862-4905 steve@stevetaubman.com

Cover Photo Credits.
Young confident businesswoman wearing
red cape against modern city background.
ShutterStock
Photo ID: 788302135
By Khakimullin Aleksandr

Overwhelmed business woman sitting at her desk
surrounded by many hands holding different objects
ShutterStock
Photo ID: 364015904
By Jason Salmon

Cataloging-in-Publication data
ISBN 13: 978-0976627111
First Edition

Praise for Dr. Taubman's Latest Work

"

A powerful book about how to thrive on life's battlefields.

"In a world where stress, chaos, discouragement and negativity are all around us, we need wisdom, honesty, and compassion to maintain our composure and rise above our challenges. My dear friend, Dr. Steve Taubman, has written a powerful book about how to thrive on life's battlefields. It's warm, wise, and packed with practical strategies for remaining calm in chaos and bringing positivity back into your life in order to achieve the life you desire."

Sharon Lechter, New York Times Bestseller
Author of Think and Grow Rich for Women
Co-author of Three Feet From Gold
Outwitting the Devil
Success and Something Greater
Rich Dad Poor Dad,...and 14 other Rich Dad titles

www.sharonlechter.com

A beautiful read...

"Beautifully written with practical steps at the end of each chapter to keep you on task for achieving higher echelons in both business & personal goals. A wonderful follow-up to "Unhypnosis."

Sarah Spencer, Host of Self Talk Radio

This book is needed more today than ever!

"Dr. Taubman takes age old philosophy and wisdom and makes it timely and relevant. Not only is there an important message, but it's easy and fun to read. Taubman hits on all the key points of focus, peak performance and, of course, happiness."

Drew Berman, Bestselling Author Founder of The Law of Collaboration International Speaker, Trainer and Coach

Too often what is commonly known as a good habit is hard to start and even harder to maintain...

"I am a long time small business advisor, and I suggest that anyone in business - especially at the smallest of size starting a business - read this book. Upon the first few chapters, I assumed this to be another often spoken prose to common sense. But take note. Too often what is commonly known as a good habit is hard to start and even harder to maintain. We all know this. And we also know that many of us fail to add, change or maintain behaviors that we once thought were simple to implement - even at the prodding of others like parents, spouses or friends.

Steve presents a simple yet formulaic recipe to gain the mental acuity one needs to perform better in business and, yes, in your personal life. This is an easy read but chock full of tidbits that you can measure against your own slate of behaviors. When I thought I had this nailed, I finished reading the book and looked back at my daily regime. I determined that I could improve myself another 25-30%. Ouch.

This alone gives one to serious thought about the tools one possesses when the next difficult situation hurls itself forward."

Tom Fleury, Business Advisor

Amazing book. Love it!

"This is a beautiful book by the gifted speaker, Dr. Steve Taubman. The five-step stress-free peak performance system is easy and actionable. Remembering to start with happiness has changed my life and I love the parable of assembling your lifeboats which can be people or whatever gives you safety in your life. This book is peppered with exercises, chapter recaps and stories that are wrappers for greater truths. Dr. Steve Taubman is brilliant and I would recommend his work for anyone who wants less stress and more happiness in their life."

J.J., Life Coach

A guidebook for staying calm...

"This is the guidebook for staying calm in the always connected 24 hours a day, 7 days a week Information Age."

Brad Szollose, Host of Awakened Nation®
Internationally known Award-winning Business Author

Dan Millman calls it "The Way of The Peaceful Warrior" Chogyam Trungpa Rinpoche calls it The Sacred Path of The Warrior...

"WHY? Why have the wisest men in the world call this sacred peaceful path a war? It's peaceful in that it's not about hurting anyone - it's about the INNER WAR! They all love using these military analogies to help prepare you for battle! And at first it's brutal - it's like being in the trenches!

It's like waking up and finding yourself in the middle of a war - and you're down in the trenches fighting for your life! Steve Taubman's Bulletproof hits the nail on the head! You have to be awake right in the midst of it all to win the war! It's like being the Buddha in the trenches!"

Barry Weiss, Meditation Coach

"I laughed, I was moved, and in one book I felt an immediate and profound impact on my professional life!"

"I laughed, I was moved, and in one book I felt an immediate and profound impact on my professional life! Too often 'business books' are dull, too systematic, and more Process Driven than is necessary. This book manages that important balance of bringing the reader into the material and providing a workable structure. And it addresses something few business books do - the need to bring harmony to the business world through mindset! Reading this book AND taking its teachings into practice will be pivotal to your future success!"

Vickie Wacek, Executive Director
BNI Vermont

Jam packed with strategies for thriving mentally and emotionally during tough times. A MUST read!

"This incredible book provides you with a proven system for managing your thoughts and emotions so that you can make the most of your skills, talents, and abilities to pursue, and achieve, your purpose and goals and leave a legacy that will far outlive you. The book is fun to read, with lots of great stories and examples that will inspire and encourage you.

Dr. Steve is not only brilliant at helping people thrive through challenges and adversity, he is also a great guy. If you have the chance to attend one of his workshops, make sure you do."

The late **Tom 'Too Tall' Cunningham,** World's most renowned Napoleon Hill Foundation Instructor Founder of Journeys To Success Radio and book series

A must read if you want more joy and ease in your life!

"Dr. Steve has created the perfect mix of inspiration and practicality. From the first few pages, I knew I had to read this engaging book with a high- lighter in hand. This is something I rarely do! I also usually race through my reading, skimming for the "good parts", not so with this one. I savored every chapter. I even look forward to reading it again! Another rarity for me! I have been reading self-help books for over 50 years now and I highly recommend this one. It is to the point, filled with real-life examples and written by a person who has walked the walk himself!"

Denise Carey, Author of A Little Book of Extraordinary Love

OUTSTANDING! Mindfulness meets motivation

"I bought this book because I got so much out of the author's first book, UnHypnosis: How to Wake Up, Start Over, and Create the Life You're Meant to Live.

"I've been recommending that one for over a year now, and this one is even better. I've never read an author that does anywhere near as good a job of weaving together the best parts of mindfulness and personal motivation. I've never left an Amazon reviews on anything else, but I did for this because I really can't speak highly enough."

Kieso, Avid fan

A clear process to rise above the stresses and distractions of our busy lives...

"Dr. Steve is a sure thing! All his work is spot on, fun to read, and impactful. In Bulletproof, he takes us through a clear process to rise above the stresses and distractions of our busy lives, and come out on top. A must-read!"

Jeff Hoffman, Global Entrepreneur
from Priceline.com and uBid.com

You'll be bulletproof!

"Be assured, when you arm yourself with the proven concepts, ideas and practices in this book, you'll be bulletproof."

Michael E. Angier, Internationally published author
President of SuccessNet

Awesome book...

"This is such an AWESOME book for those who want to take their lives to to the next level... and even for those individuals who feel that they could use a bit more AWESOME in their lives and careers!"

Speaker Erik "Mr. Awesome" Swanson
Founder of Habitude Warrior International

Valuable concepts I used to become an Olympian...

"So many valuable concepts that I used to become an Olympian...and others I wish I had known! One of the best books on mental resilience!"

Jon Horton, Three-Time Olympic Medalist
and American Ninja Warrior Star

You'll feel a renewed sense of self-confidence...

"Steve opens "Bulletproof" with a relatable childhood hero story that will capture your attention and leave you wanting more! Drawing from a lifetime of real life case studies and experiences, Steve shares the wisdom learned from working with some of the top leaders in business.

Bulletproof will help you to view your life from a new perspective, giving you the tools to release what may be holding you back and keeping you from having the life of your dreams. As you read, you'll feel a renewed sense of self-confidence growing within you."

Jordan Adler, Network Marketing Millionaire
Author of The Amazon Best Seller, "Beach Money"
Dream Broker

The definitive resource on stressfree performance...bar none!

"With the stress and uncertainty that change brings, nothing is more important than staying sane and effective under press. This book is the definitive resource on stress-free performance...bar none."

Steve Siebold, Siebold Success Network Author of How Rich People Think Mental Toughness coach

Wisdom, humor, and practical tools...

"Dr. Steve is the undisputed expert on the inner game of success. In Bulletproof, he delivers wisdom, humor, and a unique perspective on a common challenge. Every page is filled with engaging stories and relevant advice on how we can be more resilient and why we should strive for enduring happiness and significance. A sure bestseller. Buy it, read it, and buy more to give away to those you care about. My buddy Steve is changing the world and I encourage every one of us to join this remarkable man!"

Dan Clark, International Keynote Speaker Author of The Art of Significance, Puppies for Sale, and Soul Food

Dr. Steve is...helping the entire world...

"Steve is an enlightened physician dedicated to helping the entire world with his talents as a skilled entertainer and powerful communicator."

Mark Victor Hansen, *Author*
Chicken Soup for the Soul

Dedication & Acknowledgment

    This book is dedicated to all those who have inspired me and given me direction through my challenges toward a higher order of living.

    First are the saints, sages, and thought leaders who have influenced my thinking through their teachings and writings; from Jesus to Buddha, Ram Dass to Wayne Dyer, Aristotle to Eckhart Tolle, Muktananda to Alan Watts—so many enlightened souls, brilliant minds, and open hearts have touched mine, and I'm beyond grateful to each.

    Second are friends, family, and loved ones whom I've been fortunate to meet and honored to know; people who exemplify the principles in this book and hold me to a higher standard, by both example and guidance. In this category are Leonard and Arlene Taubman, my parents, who raised me with good values and a kind heart; Joan Sullivan-Taubman, my latter-day stepmom, who has shared the gift of humor as a tool to vanquish judgment; my mindfulness teacher, Barry, who constantly reminds me what it means to live honestly; and a thousand others who are floating through my mind right now. I hope they all know of their contribution to my life, of my love for them, and that if time, ink, and the patience of my readers weren't finite, they'd all be listed here.

Third is the handful of kind and generous people who gave their time and attention to this book, reading and sharing ideas to make it more relevant to you, the reader. I'm truly grateful to have such insightful, thoughtful friends who are willing to offer their wisdom without compensation.

Ultimately, my dedication is not to a person or group of people, but to an ideal and to those who embody it. If you're a sincere seeker of truth, a proponent of personal responsibility, a student of consciousness, and a responsible advocate of using your success to help humanity, this book is dedicated to you!

Table of Contents

Make-A-Wish.

Foreword

Long before **Make-a-Wish Foundation** became one of the world's most recognizable and beloved charities granting wishes to critically ill children every 34 minutes, and long before Hollywood decided to make a movie of my life, I was an Arizona Highway Patrol Motorcycle Officer. By a series of random events, I had the opportunity to help grant a wish to Chris, a 7-year old boy with leukemia, who wanted to be a Highway Patrol Motorcycle Officer like his heroes, Ponch and John from the show Chips.

That one extremely moving experience planted the seed for Make a Wish. Over the years since then, I've been very lucky to have watched thousands of caring people take ownership of this simple idea, to help suffering children experience a measure of joy, dignity and normalcy through very painful and challenging times. Watching this unfold has changed my life.

I've tried to surround myself with people who have a similar sense of mission, a desire to make a difference, and the skills to do so joyfully and artistically. **I've learned to spot those who live that mission.**

When I met Dr. Steve, I was sitting outside a high profile seminar at which I was speaking, having some lunch. It was a beautiful San Diego afternoon, and I was winding down from the long morning. Steve came by, engaged me and my assistant in some lively conversation, and shared a couple magic tricks with us... and they were good!

More than that, I got his heart. I got that here was a kindred spirit, someone with a genuine desire to bring joy and laughter to others for no other reason than that it was who he was.

Dr. Steve, I later came to find out, is a prolific author and thought leader. His words have inspired thousands to live the lives of their dreams, to overcome limiting beliefs, and to break through mental barriers to success.

In his earlier books, Steve focused on people in transition. UnHypnosis, his first book, **teaches people to get in touch with their intuition and create a life plan consistent with their values and beliefs.**

In this book, his latest, Dr. Steve shares secrets for **thriving under pressure.** Drawn from ancient wisdom and modern neuroscience, Dr. Steve offers useable ideas that can help anyone, no matter how stressed or how high pressure their lives, to stay calm in chaos, relaxed, and efficient.

This book shows you how to stay centered and be at your best even when things are at their worst. In business and life, there's nothing more important than that. Whether you're an executive, an entrepreneur, or a highway patrol officer, the way you keep your edge is by not letting your circumstances determine your mental state, and Steve does a masterful job of showing you how to do that.

When you know how to stay sane under all circumstances, you can accomplish more, enjoy your

life more, and have the bandwidth to look outside yourself to help others, change the world, and add a measure of joy and dignity to the lives of those around you. This is a message that needs to be heard, read, and implemented. This is a book that you need to read and pass on to your employees, your boss, your spouse, and your kids.

If you're like me, you'll feel Steve's heart come through every page of this life changing book, and I'm honored to help him get it the attention it deserves.

Frank Shankwitz
Creator and a Founder
Make-a-Wish Foundation

Introduction:
On Being Bulletproof

As a child of the sixties, one of my greatest joys was parking myself in front of our black-and-white Zenith television set to watch **George Reeves play Superman.** He was amazing. His understated yet confident masculinity was a thing to behold. He'd swoop into tense situations and calmly set them right. He always had that slight smirk—not enough to be obnoxious, just enough to let you know he wasn't fazed by you or anything you could throw his way.

The greatest example of that was the way he'd stand with a gentle, patient smile, hands on his hips, feet firmly planted on the ground while a villain shot him repeatedly in the chest. The bullets would bounce off, and once they finally ran out, he'd calmly walk up to the ne'er-do-well, pick him up, and fly him away to meet his inevitable fate.

What a thing. To be bulletproof. To be able to stand in the face of danger and laugh. To be completely unfazed by the threats of others. Aside from the obvious physical advantage of being immune to harm, what about the psychological impact of knowing you can't be hurt? It was astonishing!

I was not a bulletproof child. I grew up in a lot of emotional pain. I was unhappy at home, awkward, socially inept; with my glasses, braces, bad skin, greasy hair, and lack of style, the danger of being humiliated, rejected, and ignored was always present.

And those bullets went in.

That's why Superman was so profoundly appealing. He was an outsider, like me. But he felt good about himself. He could smile in the face of danger. And he'd never feel the pain of the bullets coming his way.

From childhood on, we all want to be safe, secure, and loved. We all want to be free from harm, protected from life's bullets, whether they be physical or psychological.

That desire is just as powerful in our adulthood as in our childhood, in our professional lives as in our personal lives. But now, the bullets come in many different forms. On the battlefield of life, we encounter bullets of disapproval, bullets of overwhelming demand, bullets of seemingly impossible situations that require an immediate response, bullets of crisis, and even bullets of self-criticism that we fire at ourselves. We need a method to stay calm and centered when those bullets are flying, to smile as they bounce off, or we'll succumb to the destruction they bring.

Imagine if you could laugh your way through conflict, crisis, and chaos, making split-second decisions from a place of wisdom rather than fear. Imagine if you could remain unfazed by the hostility and ignorance of others. Imagine if even the most irritating, boring, or demanding job had no power to throw you off-balance—that you could smile your slightly cocky Superman smile, do what needed to be done, and come out the other side completely unscathed!

Even under so-called "normal circumstances," our lives are stressful. We're exposed to more input than ever before. Competition is fierce. The good is separated from the great by the thinnest of lines. And for those of us in high-pressure positions, it's even more extreme. We seldom get to take a breath before we need to jump into our next challenge, and each requires just as much attention, focus, and judgment as the last. And, at least if we're living the way we were all taught, every one of our problems and crises leaves a little residue on us. It adds up. Eventually, we're buried beneath it, a heartbeat away from an ulcer, a nervous breakdown, or worse.

How many times have we watched the news and heard something like: "I don't understand it. He seemed to be such a nice, quiet young man. How could he do what he did!?"

We laugh about the term "going postal," a phrase coined after a postal worker tragically snapped and went on a murderous rampage. Clearly those people are mentally ill. But how far away from snapping are any of us? Maybe not in such a hideous and homicidal way, but how far away are we from breaking down or falling apart?

We need a new paradigm.

We long to be bulletproof, immune to the pressures of life, not guarded and shut off, or living behind armor that lets nothing in, but keeping a semi-permeable membrane between us and the world. Love gets in. Joy gets in. Compassion gets in. But aggravation, frustration, abuse ... they all bounce off.

Maybe you're thinking that's impossible or you have to take the bad with the good, but I want to inspire you to open your mind. Yes, maybe you do have to take the bad with the good. But you don't have to take it to heart. You have a choice of how deep it goes. You don't have to bury your head in the sand or ignore reality in order to choose a better mindset.

My intention is to show you what I've been learning from a more than thirty-year journey of self-discovery, validated by scientific research and ancient wisdom. As it turns out, there are powerful things you can do to thrive in a world fraught with bullets, things that don't require you to shut down or run away to be safe and happy.

If you knew those things, how much better would you perform under pressure? Freed of the burden of fear, would you be more courageous? Freed of the burden of insult, would you be more compassionate? Freed of the burden of feeling overwhelmed, would you be more persistent?

The five-step system presented in this book has a kind of magic to it. Whereas making physical changes, such as losing weight, can be a tedious and time-dependent process, the stress-releasing mindfulness techniques herein are transformational; they can produce profound changes in your sense of well-being instantly. Many of the ideas you read in the following pages will produce shifts in your awareness, your priorities, and worldview. As these ideas resonate within your deeper mind, the truth of their teachings will be instantly obvious, as if you were remembering something long forgotten. As they take root in the fertile soil of your subconscious, you'll begin to adjust how you feel and act, immediately and with little effort.

This book is an invitation to change your relationship with conflict, stress, and fear. By learning the skills in this book, you'll work more productively, remain calm in crises, and exude an energy of happiness that attracts others to you. You'll refine your leadership qualities, improve your sales, or simply rise above the stress of a chaotic job. You'll improve your relationships, act wisely, inspire confidence, and develop an unshakeable sense of inner peace, even when the bullets are flying!

"A warrior's mind and body must be permeated with enlightened wisdom and deep calm."

- Morihei Ueshiba, founder of Aikido

Chapter One:
The Pressure of Life As We Know It

*"Diamonds are nothing more than chunks of coal
that stuck to their jobs."*
—Malcolm Forbes

At the bottom of the Mariana Trench, seven miles below the surface of the ocean, pressure measures about a thousand times that on land. Picture a thousand people your size sitting on top of you. If you were down there, you'd be crushed instantly. So would a bank safe.

Yet there are animals thriving down there. The largest are foot-long shrimp-like creatures called amphipods, but they're far from alone. Dozens of species thrive in the deep.

Here on dry land, there are many extremely high-pressure environments: hospitals, board rooms, crime scenes, government offices, and perhaps your workplace. In each of these places are unusual creatures who thrive. Meanwhile, to one degree or another, many others are crushed daily. Not physically, but psychologically and spiritually.

If you're among them, you know the pressure all too well! Deadlines, crises, relentless initiatives, bottomless inboxes, absurd workloads, and so on. Or maybe your pressure is interpersonal: the demanding boss, the competitive co-worker, the climate of suspicion, the every-man-for-himself culture, or the lack of appreciation. For most of us, it's a bit of both.

To thrive under such conditions requires a different set of skills, ones most of us lack. Which is why we as a society suffer from an unprecedented incidence of stress-related illness. While in days gone by, it was common to die from infectious diseases that had no cure, most of us in the so-called civilized world today instead succumb to cancer, diabetes, heart disease, stroke, and a host of other preventable disorders. Almost all of the top killers that claim our lives are lifestyle-related and traceable to things like stress, poor dietary habits, lack of exercise, lack of attention, and exposure to a toxic environment.

And if these diseases don't kill you, the circumstances under which they thrive will most likely diminish your effectiveness. We now know that high-pressure situations, when not met with the proper skill set, lead to poor work output, high levels of burnout, employee turnover, low job satisfaction, and perhaps even mental illness. And now, **we're becoming increasingly aware that unhappy employees are less productive,** more likely to repel customers, and prone to spread their negativity to those around them.

If you're in a high-pressure situation, your ability to meet it effectively will determine your level of success, the quality of your relationships, and the degree of well-being you get to enjoy. And, if your high-pressure job involves helping or influencing others, there's a strong likelihood that your inability to bear the pressure is diminishing your capacity to do both.

According to a 2000 study by Integra, reported in an article from the American Institute of Stress:

- 65% of workers say **workplace stress** has caused difficulties, and more than **10%** describe these as having **major effects**
- 10% say they work in an atmosphere where **physical violence has occurred because of job stress,** and in this group; **42% report that yelling** and other **verbal abuse** is common
- **29% have yelled at co-workers** because of workplace stress; **14% say they work where machinery or equipment has been damaged** because of workplace rage; and 2% admit that they have **actually personally struck someone**
- **19%, or almost one in five respondents, have quit a previous position because of job stress,** and nearly one in four have been driven to tears because of workplace stress
- **62% routinely find that their day ended with work-related neck pain; 44% report stressed-out eyes, 38% complain of pain in their hands;** and **34% report difficulty in sleeping,** all due to stress.
- **12% have called in sick** because of job stress
- Over half say they often spend **12-hour days on work-related duties** and an equal number **frequently skip lunch** because of he stress of job demands

These statistics are highly troubling and might lead one to conclude that it's a hopeless situation. Obviously, with such a pervasive problem, the system itself is flawed, and surviving, let alone thriving, is perhaps too much to expect.

Bear in mind, that study was done more than 15 years ago. Things have only gotten worse. The world has become increasingly stressful. We're drowning in data. According to Dr. Martin Hilbert at the University of Southern California, there are 295 exabytes of data floating around cyberspace; that's 315 times the number of grains of sand on the earth. We receive more input in a week than our grandparents did in their entire lives … and it's overwhelming.

Some 44 percent of Americans report they are less happy than five years ago.

Just look at the increased use of anxiety meds and the spike in stress-related illnesses. Chances are, you or someone you care about has been affected by a stress-related illness, such as heart disease, stroke, cancer, obesity, eating disorders, sleeping disorders, or even opiate addiction.

Depressing indeed! But, if this were our inevitable fate, there would be no one among us who would thrive in times of stress. Yet we know there are some who do. And I'm not talking about unconscious workaholics who press on in spite of stress, thinking they're at the top of their game while ulcers and heart disease are lurking in the shadows. I'm talking about human amphipods—people who are legitimately at peace and effective under the same stress and pressure that do most people in.

People like "Wild Bill."

Not long ago, I had the good fortune to connect with a gentleman named Art who read about my work and felt moved to reach out to me. He shared a story he'd heard about a World War II survivor nicknamed Wild Bill. Here's that story in Art's words...

"The time was May 1945 at the end of World War II. The scene was a Nazi concentration camp. George G. Ritchie, who later became an M.D., was part of the 123rd Evac. George was there to help get medical supplies to the newly liberated prisoners and process them for release. The camp was near Wuppertal, Germany; the American soldiers found a man and gave him the name Wild Bill Cody because he had a long, drooping handlebar mustache.

It was obvious to George and the other soldiers that Wild Bill had not been there very long; his posture was erect, his eyes were bright and his energy was indefatigable. He was fluent in English, French, German, and Russian, as well as Polish, and he became the unofficial camp translator. He helped George and the other soldiers 15 to 16 hours a day with release paperwork, without showing signs of weariness.

While everyone else was fatigued, Bill would say: These people have waited all day for our help. And George would even come to Wild Bill when his spirits were low. The camp had inmates from nationalities that hated one another almost as much as they hated the Germans, yet Wild Bill was liked by all of them and was chosen to help mediate their disputes. Over the weeks they worked together on liberating the camp, Bill became their greatest asset..."

Art wondered how Wild Bill had become such an unusual man who had managed not just to survive the concentration camp, **but to thrive in it.** In fact, Art

The question is, if it's possible to thrive in brutal captivity, isn't it possible to do so in an imperfect work situation?

coined the term thriver to describe him.

None of us, I hope, will ever experience the horror of a concentration camp; yet all of us face our own challenges. The question is, if it's possible to thrive in brutal captivity, why isn't it possible to do so in an imperfect work situation?

Granted, our system is broken. **We've created a world in which success has been redefined to mean making money at the expense of well-being.** The relentless pursuit of personal wealth or the demand to do more with less in service to corporate objectives is not healthy. Wisdom demands that we evaluate our situations and choose those that best serve our greater needs—balancing our need for money with our need for personal satisfaction, healthy relationships, a feeling of accomplishment, a sense of belonging, and a knowledge that we're making a contribution in the world.

But life is a series of compromises, and while we'd all like to work in an environment that is nurturing and rewarding at all levels, sometimes the best we can hope for is a position that doesn't drive us insane or exceed our ability to survive the demands and expectations before us. Maybe, if we choose wisely, we'll end up somewhere that does a pretty good job of letting us succeed in a satisfying way. And then, within that environment, our objective is to make the most of our less-than-ideal situation and use it as *"grist for the mill."* In other words, to take a merely tolerable situation and turn it into the canvas on which we paint our masterpiece.

So, yes, many of us have very stressful jobs. Yes, many of us are under almost relentless pressure. And yes, many of us might do better to consider a different option than the one we've chosen. But most of us, whether out of necessity, habit, a sense of mission, dogged determination, or discomfort with change, are unlikely to leave our current jobs. So the question becomes: How do I make the most of this situation?

For many, that question comes with a supposition, that there's no way to actually end up liking this, so the best I can do is figure out how not to become sick and miserable.

But what if even more were possible? What if you could, like the amphipod, learn to do more than just avoid being crushed under the pressure? What if you could literally thrive under difficult circumstances? What if this burden you've been carrying were to suddenly become an engine pushing you upward and onward? What if there were a way to distinguish yourself as one of the rare few who perform at your best in the midst of pressure?

What if this burden you've been carrying were to suddenly become an engine pushing you upward and onward?

Imagine the impact you could have, the power you'd feel, the success you'd enjoy ... if you were truly at home in the trenches, the battle raging on around you while you made calm and deliberate choices, moved courageously across the field of battle, and planted your flag on the highest hill, all the while with that Superman-like smirk of knowing that you're safe.

I'm reminded here of Dan Millman's wonderful book *The Way of the Peaceful Warrior*. What we're talking about here is nothing less than a personal transformation that will allow you to remain peaceful while wielding your power and fighting the battles of your personal and professional life—a warrior with a wise mind, an open heart, and a sense of humor.

If you work for yourself, such an attitude will give you the courage to try new things, to set bigger goals, and to envision a greater future—perhaps one in which you're making a mark on the world. If you work for someone else, that transformation will enhance your mastery; it will mark a noticeable shift that will attract your superiors to you and influence your upward mobility. And, if you're a leader, your capacity for calm and competence in the face of pressure will inspire your team and probably invite greater engagement and enthusiasm.

So, unless you're committed to leaving your current situation, this book is going to be very important for you. Because you're going to learn how to shift your mindset in such a way that you're able to thrive in high-pressure situations and enjoy all the benefits that thriving brings.

If you're ready to take on the challenge of planting your flag high above the battlefield of your life, read on. In the next chapter, we'll outline the basic five-step battle plan that will have you operating at a much higher level of effectiveness and a much lower level of stress ... laughing your way to the bank and inspiring others to grow and change. I have absolute faith in your ability to be do this, and I'm committed to your well-being. **Join me now to learn the "secret skills" that distinguish high-pressure thrivers from survivors and victims!**

Important points from Chapter One:

- We exist under tremendous pressure
- Some creatures thrive under such conditions
- We may choose to leave our high-pressure situations
- Or we can choose to become "thrivers"
- Our transformation benefits us and the world around us

Chapter Two:
The Five-Step Stress-Free Peak Performance System:
An Overview

"I accept life unconditionally. Most people ask for happiness on condition. Happiness can only be felt if you don't set any condition."

—Arthur Rubinstein, Conductor

As my mindfulness coach friend Barry likes to say, *"Your issues are not the issue."* We've been raised to believe that the circumstances surrounding us—our jobs, our family, our friends and our adversaries—determine our happiness or lack thereof. In fact, that point of view is so deeply ingrained that we don't stop to question it. Of course I'm unhappy! Did you get a look at my husband??? Naturally I'm miserable. I've got a boss who won't shut up! How could you possibly expect me to be happy with the economy in the tank!?

All this flies in the face of what we now know about happiness and success. Our emotional well-being and our prosperity are largely determined by our thoughts and our emotions, not our jobs, our relationships, our circumstances of birth, or luck.

This should come as good news, because if our success and happiness are indeed determined by our internal state, there's hope of changing them. If, on the other hand, our happiness and success are determined by what's happening around us or by the actions of others, we're powerless to change how we feel or what we accomplish.

That doesn't stop us from trying, though! Without consciously realizing it, we live under the assumption that something outside of ourselves is at fault whenever we're dissatisfied, frustrated, irritated, or depressed. The logical solution to our misery, therefore, is to try to change the other person or the circumstance in which we find ourselves. If only I could get you, my irritating employee, to shape up, then I could be happy and stop grumbling and complaining.

The problem with this approach is that we have little if any control over things outside ourselves.

So, we doom ourselves to misery. If I need you to change so I can be happy, and it's almost impossible to get you to change, logic dictates that I'll almost never be happy.

And if I'm almost never happy, I'm also almost never successful. Because research now proves that my inner state is the best determinant of my success. The field of positive psychology has turned the entire happiness paradigm on its ear. More on that later.

What all that boils down to is that, as Barry put it, your issues are not the issue. Your insistence that they are is the basis of your misery. You don't really need to solve your issues to be happy. The real issue is you. How are you handling what comes your way?

In order to accomplish the goal of this book—to perform at peak levels without stress in high-pressure situations—you'll first need to embrace this concept. You are the author of your fate. You are the reason you're happy or miserable. And you have the power to change it.

To accomplish this shift, I've developed a five-part formula that we'll explore over the next several chapters. By embracing each of these parts, you'll develop an arsenal of psychological tools to release your grip on suffering, experience emotional freedom, and pursue your tasks with greater enthusiasm, optimism, and gratitude. And, in so doing, you'll find yourself becoming more influential, more creative, and more productive. You'll get more done in less time and produce more substantive changes than ever before, leading to greater prosperity and inner peace.

As you'll see, each of the five parts builds on the one before, and together they'll give you an arsenal of unimaginable power. It's also perhaps valuable to share that these principles have been vetted over thousands of years and multiple cultures. You'll find references to them in Christianity, Buddhism, Judaism, and Islam. You'll see them validated in experiments conducted at Harvard, Yale, Stanford, and other prestigious institutes. You'll find them being used as the foundation for success in athletics, warfare, medicine, and business. And above all else, after giving them just a relatively short but sincere trial, you'll be able to prove to yourself their worth and value.

Once you've come to understand the foundation for peak performance in Chapters Three through Seven, we'll apply them in Chapter Eight, along with some pretty slick life hacks, to the specific challenges of high-pressure situations. That's when we'll look at practical action steps you can take when faced with deadlines, interpersonal conflict, crisis, feeling overwhelmed, and the like.

For now, let's lay out the five-part formula for stress-free peak performance, each part of which will have its own chapter.

Chapters 3–7: The Five Steps

1. Start with happiness.
In Chapter Three, we'll explore the notion that happiness must be your starting point. Nothing of any value will come from a life lived without this awareness.
There are several reasons one might think otherwise:
First, most of us have been raised in a puritanical paradigm that says work is not meant to be enjoyed.

Second, most of us have been programmed to believe that happiness is the byproduct of achieving our goals and getting what we want, rather than the other way around.

Third, most of us simply never think about it. We're too busy struggling to get ahead to even wonder why we're doing it.

In this chapter, we'll take all that apart and start again.

2. Clean up your act (outside and in).
In Chapter Four, we'll explore all the ways you've created unnecessary stress and struggle in your work and home life. We'll dig into the universal effects of integrity, impeccability, and morality. We'll look at how you've organized the world around you and see how disorder and disarray might be limiting your potential. We'll discuss the importance of living by a code of conduct. I'll invite you to take a hard but dispassionate look at yourself and gauge your levels

of consistency, responsibility, and accountability. And, we'll develop a plan to help you bring greater order and basic goodness to your life. You'll create a series of rituals— unbreakable contracts that you'll use to increase trust in yourself, your personal power, and your integrity.

3. Sharpen your focus.

In Chapter Five, we'll begin to build a new understanding that has, until recently, completely eluded the Western world. You'll learn how Eastern traditions have viewed religious beliefs as merely the first step in a much more powerful and valuable journey, involving the deliberate and systematic exercise of our ability to focus. And you'll learn how, through modern technology, neuroscientists are now proving the truth of those ancient principles. Our minds are malleable. We can change our thinking. Focus-based exercises can change how your brain functions, and in taking on those exercises, you can expect to become smarter, happier, more compassionate, and less affected by the circumstances surrounding you. By the end of this chapter, you'll have a clear, simple-to-execute strategy for sharpening your focus.

4. Lean in to the pressure.

In Chapter Six, you'll make another paradigm shift, from avoiding things you don't like to embracing them. In our lives, we've all come to naturally move toward pleasure and away from pain. Hence, our experience of handling unpleasant circumstances is one of avoidance. We hate feeling uncomfortable, so we run from situations that produce discomfort. And, in so doing, we deprive ourselves of the wisdom we might gain if we were to stay and meet those situations with equanimity and calm acceptance. The focus exercises of the previous chapter will give you a new perspective on discomfort, and as a result, you'll be able to lean into pain and pressure without suffering. In fact, you'll learn deeply and experientially that there's a difference between pain and suffering. As Haruki Murakami said, "Pain is inevitable. Suffering is optional." Once you internalize this lesson, you'll become bulletproof: capable of withstanding conflict and transforming difficult situations into giant wins.

5. Assemble your lifeboats.

In Chapter Seven, we'll explore the notion of necessary strength. Each of us is somewhere on a continuum from completely unconscious to enlightened.

Another way to say that is that some of us are powerlifters with incredible strength to meet our challenges, while others are ninety-pound weaklings who collapse at the first sign of conflict or pressure. While it might seem that where you are on that continuum says something about you as a person, that's not the case. Each of us has the capacity to move further along that line, growing in consciousness and in our ability to control our own minds.

However, along the way, we need help. Until you're completely enlightened, you'll find yourself in situations beyond your current ability to handle. You may find yourself drowning in a given circumstance. That's because you're not yet strong enough for that challenge. Which is fine. That's why you need to have your lifeboats assembled. You need people and systems in place to protect you and help you move elegantly through those tough times. You need to train your friends on how to support you and how to know when you need that support. You need to know what to do when you feel yourself coming unglued. Once you've prepared for the worst, you'll feel greater confidence in facing difficult situations.

The more you face them appropriately, the more strength you'll gain and the less need you'll have for those lifeboats.

As we make our way through the five parts of the **Stress Free Peak Performance Formula (SFPPF),** you'll want to evaluate your current state and try to see yourself through objective eyes. At times, you'll find it helps to invite someone else to give you that objective perspective, so I'd encourage you to have a study partner moving forward.

Find a trusted friend with whom you can share your insights and discoveries, one with whom you're comfortable being honest and vulnerable. A supportive partner won't try to fix you or change you. They won't try to correct you or buy into your negativity. For example, if you share your frustration about a given person or situation, you'll want your support partner not to agree that the other person or circumstance is bad or wrong. Instead, you'll want your partner to reflect back to you what you're feeling and encourage you to go deeper. *"I hear you're really frustrated about your boss. What are your choices at this point?"*

Until you've gained the strength and wisdom to see yourself clearly, it'll be of huge help to have a friend (or a community) who can see you more clearly than you can see yourself.

All you need at this point is a commitment. Remind yourself why you're reading this book. It's easy to justify your aggravation about those around you, so you can expect that your mind will put up a lot of resistance to concepts in this book that may seem counterintuitive. There will be many times when you're convinced that you're right and others are wrong—and that making them see that is of paramount importance. In other words, there will be many times when you lose sight of the lesson and come to believe, maybe even insist, that the issue is the issue.

Are you willing to push through that, to question your version of reality, and to accept the notion that your strength often lies in your ability not to react but rather to use your challenges as opportunities for growth and insight?

The greatest thing you can remind yourself about upon experiencing resistance, right now and forever, is this: You are NOT your mind! DON'T believe everything you think! The question is: Are you open to exploring that perspective? If so, let's move forward and begin developing new habits, the habits of peak performers who sail through conflict and crisis to create a more desirable situation ... and a better world!

Important points from Chapter Two:
- Your mind, not your circumstances, determines your success and happiness
- Happiness must precede success, not the other way around; happiness is a goal unto itself
- You'll need to establish a foundation of order and integrity before moving on
- Beyond religious beliefs and rules of conduct, you must develop your focus
- With focus, you'll gain the wisdom to change your relationship with discomfort
- As you work toward greater inner strength, having

Note from the author:

Throughout this book and at the end of chapters 3-7, you'll be offered a series of exercises to help you get the most out of the ideas presented. I recommend that you have a journal or notebook handy for completing the exercises and capturing your thoughts as you go along.

To begin, realize that it's virtually impossible to create powerful and lasting change until you can **recognize and accept your current situation.** Toward that end, stop and take a mental inventory of your life as it is right now. *What works? What doesn't work? How much of your discontent is generated by your outer circumstances? How much is just a feeling from within?*

How would you rate yourself in the areas of **energy, enthusiasm, optimism,** and **focus?** What would it mean for you to increase your scores in each of those areas?

Finally, are you open to change? Are you willing to try on a new set of attitudes, skills, and habits?

After exploring these questions and reflecting on your answers, read on, and we'll begin to assemble your battle plan for a life of greater ease and mastery.

Chapter Three:
Start With Happiness

"I accept life unconditionally. Most people ask for happiness on condition. Happiness can only be felt if you don't set any condition."
—Arthur Rubinstein, Conductor

"The purpose of life is to be happy."
—The Dalai Lama, spiritual leader

"I'm gonna die with a smile if it kills me."
—Jon Gailmor, American folk singer

Consistent peak performance is not possible without happiness. Sure, you can exert effort and force, and for a while you'll perform at high levels, but you won't be able to sustain it. Your results will waver, and more importantly, you'll start to crack.

There is now a large body of research available under the heading of positive psychology. Serious scientists, psychologists, neurologists, and clinicians have been studying the effects of happiness on success for over twenty years. That's to say nothing of the millennia of empirical observations on the topic or the teachings of positive thinking in the literature of the past hundred years.

What's different now and what makes this such an exciting time is that we finally have proof. This is, as my positive psychology trainer friend Don Sandel says, no longer a "soft skill." Magnetic resonance imaging and other relatively new technologies allow us to glimpse the brain as it experiences different states of consciousness, and statistical data has been compiled about the relationship between happiness and productivity, health, and financial success, among other things.

Among the many intriguing findings from the current research, it's now been proven that happy employees are ...

- **85% more efficient at their work**
- **10 times less likely to take sick leave**
- **50% better at getting things done**

Further, it's been found that those who found purpose in their work experience a...

- **60% drop in absenteeism**
- **75% reduction in turnover**

A multi-industry study of six companies found that, on average, a thriving [happy, engaged], workplace increases performance by 16%.

The conclusion? We need to be happy to be competent, productive and successful.

And yet, how often do we delay happiness in an effort to attain a goal that we believe will make us happy? How often do we use effort, stress, and obsessive energy to try to accomplish that goal, refusing to feel anything but stern resolve? We lose ourselves in the serious pursuit of our objectives and forget that we're human beings, entitled to a joyful experience now.

The irony is that we're more productive, creative, and motivated when we're happy, so any effort to succeed without happiness is at best inefficient and at worst a complete waste.

Why is it that this is so profoundly easy to ignore? If there's truth to the assertion that happiness causes success (and there is), how is it that we continue to treat happiness as the byproduct of accomplishment rather than its prerequisite?

Programming

We've been deeply programmed—I would assert, hypnotized—over the course of our lifetimes to link happiness to accomplishment. We're so completely indoctrinated into that point of view that we're blind to the truth.

Let's look at your experience. Perhaps, when you were seventeen years old, you longed for your own car. You knew that once you had it, you would be happy. Nothing could be more important than that car. You would willingly wallow in misery until it became a reality. Eventually, you got that car. And indeed, you were ecstatic. How long did that feeling last? A day? A week? How long before you found another thing you had to have before you could be happy again? And once you got that, how long were you happy then?

What is it that you need now? A new house? A better car? A vacation? Are you certain that will make you happy? Are you deeply longing for that thing? Are you stressing out about getting it? And once you do, how long do you imagine you'll stay happy this time? Probably not long!

And yet, we continue living as if something outside of us will bring us happiness. It is the very definition of hypnosis that we're unable to see any reality that contradicts our existing programmed beliefs. As long as you continue to live with the mental program that happiness is externally derived, you will completely overlook the hideous track record of that strategy.

As long as you continue to live with the mental program that happiness is externally derived, you will completely overlook the hideous track record of that strategy.

Highly successful people start with happiness. They set goals while happy. Happiness is the fountain from which their creativity arises. They envision the outcome of that goal regularly because the vision makes them happy. They live in their future reality as a way of evoking the state of happiness that drives them forward. They evolve a strategy for achievement that takes into account the condition of happiness.

They may set lofty and seemingly unattainable goals, holding themselves to a high standard and imagining great things beyond their current capabilities, but they do so with an understanding that attainment, or lack thereof, isn't the source of their happiness. The quest itself is fulfilling, and the energy behind that quest is always of a positive nature.

Compare that with the obsessive, dour, overly serious energy of someone driven by need rather than passion. From the outside, passion and obsession may look the same; both result in persistent action. But passionate individuals undertake the work joyfully and feel an inner energy that drives them forward and replenishes them. The obsessive person is driven by fear, shame, and obligation. The energy of obsession is destructive and depleting, and ultimately burns them out.

Developing the self-awareness to notice if and when you slip from passion to obsession, as we're all inclined to do from time to time, is vital. When we explore the topic of focus in Chapter Five, you'll learn how to develop that self-awareness. For now, resolve to make happiness a priority, meaning: commit yourself to cultivating happiness in every moment, despite where you are, what you're doing, or who you're with.

Let's get practical. What does positive psychology have to tell us about the art of happiness? What are some specific, practical, and reliable tools to create a happier perspective? What can you do right now, what habits can you change immediately, that will begin to make you a happier person, free of stress and immune to pressure?

Here is a list of the most effective catalysts known for creating unconditional happiness.

1. Reject conditional happiness

Stop thinking that achieving a goal will provide anything other than momentary satisfaction. Choose to stop using accomplishment as your happiness strategy. Practice letting go of demands and expectations that you've tied to your happiness. Learn to make it OK that the world isn't currently conforming to your view of how it should be. If you want, borrow the parental mantra, "I get what I get and I don't get upset!" The more you can challenge the idea that things need to be a certain way for you to be happy, the more personal power you'll feel and the more balanced you'll become in high-pressure situations. After all, if you're busy fighting reality, how can you apply wisdom and judgment to your current situation? Try looking at every unwanted situation as an opportunity to practice rising above your demands and expectations. It's OK to have preferences; just don't insist they're always met.

2. Express gratitude

Studies show that one of the most powerful tools for shifting your mindset to one of happiness is gratitude. According to a research review published in the Harvard Medical School newsletter, two psychological studies found a powerful link between gratitude, optimism, and happiness. In one study, students who were asked to make "gratitude lists" had significant improvements in optimism after ten weeks. In another study, students who were asked to write a letter of gratitude to someone in their lives who had not been properly thanked "immediately had a huge increase in happiness scores." In fact, no other intervention came close to creating these dramatic changes in happiness. Other studies found a link between gratitude and improved relationships, both business and personal. Simple ways to cultivate gratitude, according to the Harvard newsletter, include making daily gratitude lists, sending "at least one gratitude letter per month, once in a while to yourself," thanking someone mentally, and keeping a gratitude journal.

3. Take care of yourself

The body-mind connection is undeniable. If you're depleted physically, that will show up in your stamina, your attitudes, your patience, and your mental resilience. Simple practices like eating well, drinking plenty of water, exercising, maintaining good spinal alignment, getting adequate sleep, standing up straight, and breathing deeply all contribute to your sense of well-being. If you're not feeling energetic, alive, and happy, investigate whether you're ignoring one or more of these powerful catalysts, and take action. Another interesting physical health-related consideration is the balance of your neurohormones, which influence your sense of well-being. In the book The Mood Cure, Julia Ross suggests several dietary changes and supplements that might influence the production and release of mood-enhancing neurohormones.

4. Change the narrative

How we interpret situations in our lives has a much greater impact on our well-being than the situations themselves. Many of the things that happen to us daily are capable of being viewed in various ways. Most of the circumstances which we give a negative spin or story can be spun in an entirely different way. An optimist will look at a challenge as an opportunity. A pessimist might see the same exact situation as proof that life is just too hard. If you find yourself judging your experiences in a negative way, consider changing the story you're telling yourself. Remember the story of the twins who, on their birthday, are shown into a room full of horse manure. The pessimistic kid runs out crying. The optimistic one grabs a shovel and starts digging, saying, "There must be a pony in here somewhere!" Practice finding the pony under every pile of manure in your life, and it won't be long before you actually dig one out.

5. Nurture your relationships

Harvard University researchers conducted a 75-year study following individuals throughout their lifetimes to determine what made them happy. At the end of one of the longest and most exhaustive research projects ever, it was clear that money, power, and influence were not great predictors of happiness. Relationships were. Robert Waldinger, the current study director, put it simply. "The clearest message we get from this 75-year study is this: Good relationships keep us happier and healthier. Period." If that's the case, we need to dedicate more time, more presence, and more reverence to our relationships. Qualities such as honesty, authenticity, vulnerability, and generosity must be prioritized, cultivated, and cherished. Avoid the mistake that so many in high-pressure situations make: don't take your friends and family for granted. They're a big part of what keeps you functioning well in the world.

6. Find the funny

It's long been known that laughter has a profound impact on our attitudes, worldview, health, and happiness. Most people know the story of Dr. Norman Cousins, author of Anatomy of an Illness, who used funny movies to combat the pain and dysfunction of his disease, ankylosing spondylitis. As early as 1996, a body of research already existed on the impact of laughter. Psychology Today reported that neuroscientists found laughter to be a "full cortical experience," meaning it affects the entire brain in a positive way. MRI and PET imagery show substantial changes during

In fact, "forced laughter" will eventually have you laughing for real...

laughter. Interestingly, it turns out that you don't actually need something funny to happen to get the benefits of laughter. You can just start laughing and still experience the same positive effects. In fact, "forced laughter" will eventually have you laughing for real, releasing all sorts of performance-enhancing drugs into your brain. Bottom line: Laughter is serious business. Don't ignore it.

7. Monitor your thinking

Our greatest gift and our greatest opportunity is self-awareness. Socrates said, "Know thyself." The field of cognitive therapy is based on the notion that our unhappiness is caused largely by our unresourceful thinking. The problem is that we seldom stop to look at what we're thinking. Our most powerful thoughts go unexamined and therefore unchallenged. Get in the habit of watching yourself think. Notice that if you're in a bad mood, chances are there's a series of thoughts playing in the background, like the background music in a movie, that are sustaining that mood. Instead of doing their bidding and keeping your attention focused on the problem on which your thoughts are riveted, try to fix the mood before you fix the mess. In other words, take the time to notice the background thoughts, correct them, and arrive in a more centered, calm place before you try to fix that problem. Often, once you fix the mood, you'll find the mess has magically vanished, because how we see things is often the problem, not the things themselves. One specific area of unconscious thinking that requires deliberate attention is forgiveness. If you're carrying around resentment or anger toward another person, it's taking up unwanted space in your brain and producing chemical reactions that are making you less effective. Monitor your resentful thinking and try to let it go. It's in your best interest.

8. Practice mindfulness

We'll be looking much more deeply at this in Chapter Five, but it's important to recognize the importance of mindfulness as it applies to happiness. Research shows that even brief periods of mindfulness meditation will trigger profound neurological and hormonal changes in your brain. The practice of nonjudgmental awareness—the basis of mindfulness—has more physical and mental benefits than virtually any other practice known to man. In regard to happiness, meditating just five minutes twice per day will increase your sense of well-being, calm, and compassion, while awakening the experience of joy in you. Set aside between five and twenty minutes in the morning and evening for mindfulness practice. Sit quietly in a private place where you will not be disturbed, and just observe your breath. Allow thoughts to arise and pass. If you find your mind wandering, don't make the mistake of thinking, this isn't working. Just commit the time and let your thoughts settle of their own accord. Again, we'll go into greater depth on this later, but know now that mindfulness is a powerful key to happiness, especially if you're encountering high-pressure situations that demand focus

9. Surround yourself with positive people

Jim Rohn used to say, *"You're the average of the five people you spend most of your time with."* If those people are negative, pessimistic people, you're likely to become one yourself. If you deliberately put yourself in the company of optimists, it will become very difficult to maintain your pessimistic attitude. Understand that neither attitude is inherently right or wrong, true or false. You can make a case for either one. The question is: Which is more resourceful? Which attitude is more conducive to functioning well in the world? Which will make you happier?

Often, pessimists view optimists as naive or stupid. They suppose that if optimists saw things as clearly as they, they'd have no choice but to become pessimists. But that's not the case. Optimists have all the same information and choose to come to a different conclusion, not out of intellectual dishonesty but out of a wise understanding of the value of a positive mindset. If you tend to see things from a negative standpoint, try to release your sense of righteousness and surround yourself with positive people. It won't be long before you realize they know what they are doing!

Here's a story from my editor, Doreen:

"My husband is one of those people who secretly believes that if, in any situation, you spend time worrying about the worst-case scenario, you will prevent it from happening. He takes a pessimistic view of just about everything, for example whether we're going to get to the event we're headed to on time during rush hour. He accuses me of being too optimistic about everything (and now and then, being late as a result!).

We've been married 30 years, and this has been a constant refrain. One day recently I said: Okay, you can mentally prepare for the worst if you want, but do you ever prepare for the best to happen? He realized he never does that! Somehow it clicked with him and he decided he'd try preparing for the best for a while and see what happened. Days later he started out on a trip on a standby ticket, readily got a premium seat without even asking for it, had a great, encouraging visit with our daughter (who'd recently had some struggles), made a bunch of new friends, was a huge success at the event where he was coaching, got back home on a ferry and another standby ticket without trouble, and everything fell into place beautifully. He came back from what might have been a stressful trip feeling like he'd had a vacation. He said it felt remarkably freeing not to be thinking all the time about when the other shoe was going to drop. He felt he could enjoy the moment. The power of a positive mindset, indeed!"

10. Become a hugger

Thirty years ago, in my previous life as a chiropractor, I attended a practice management symposium where I met Dr. Joe Charbonneau, one of the most respected motivational speakers in history. Joe used to say, *"You need three hugs a day just to be healthy, and ten to grow!"* Virginia Satir also said something very similar. "We need four hugs a day for survival. We need eight hugs a day for maintenance. We need twelve hugs a day for growth." Granted, there was no science behind those statements at the time, but it made me and others happy, so I took them at their word. Now, the research is there. For example, hugging causes the release of the neurohormone oxytocin, which not only makes us feel loved but reverses the effects of stress, such as elevated blood pressure. Children who are touch-deprived and don't receive hugs regularly experience delays in talking, walking, and reading. According to Happiness Weekly, a full-body hug stimulates your nervous system while decreasing feelings of loneliness, combating fear, increasing self-esteem, defusing tension, and showing appreciation. If you want to grow, to thrive, and to give a powerful gift to others, consider finding appropriate ways to offer hugs.

11. Dedicate yourself to a higher purpose

Psychology Today published an excellent article a few years ago titled *"The Power of Purpose."* The author argues that people who have a sense of purpose are healthier, happier, and more resistant to the effects of stress. He says, "aligning ourselves to a purpose often makes us less self-centered. We feel a part of something bigger, something outside ourselves, and this makes us less focused on our own worries and anxieties. Our own problems seem less significant, and we spend less time thinking about them, and so our sense of well-being increases." Victor Frankl, author of Man's Search for Meaning, survived in the concentration camps by having a purpose greater than himself. And Wild Bill, the holocaust thriver mentioned earlier in this book, made himself vital to those around him by choosing to actively embrace love over hate, even after he witnessed his wife and children killed in front of him. He simply refused to give in to hatred or fear, but instead chose to use his experience as an opportunity to live out the purpose of loving others. What can you dedicate yourself to? Consider that, and keep the awareness of the purpose you've chosen in the forefront of your mind. You'll be happier and more effective.

12. Ask the right questions

It used to be the rage to say "affirmations," positive statements about yourself: "I'm good enough, I'm smart enough, and doggone it, people like me!" But it's become clear that statements we make with our conscious minds are often refuted by our subconscious minds. So, you say, *"I'm great!"* And your sub-conscious says, *"No, you're not!"* But ... questions are powerful. Ask yourself: *What's great about me?* And your subconscious will go to work trying to find an-swers to that question. Chances are, if you're feeling depressed, anxious, overwhelmed, or insecure, you're probably asking yourself the wrong questions. Take note whether you're asking yourself things like, What's wrong with me? or What else can go wrong? If you are, your subconscious mind is only too happy to answer you! The right questions are those that invite positive answers. So, a daily practice of deliberately asking good questions will change the way you feel. Try starting your day with a question like: What are ten good reasons that what I'm doing is of value in the world? Or: In what ways am I demonstrating my most positive values? If you do this daily and write down your answers, you'll begin to feel immediately better, more optimistic, and eager to meet your challenges.

13. Practice wonder and awe
The latest arrival on the field of happiness research is wonder. Seeing the world through the eyes of a child—practicing what Zen monks call "beginner's mind"—has a profound effect on happiness and productivity. Among other things, the literature now proves that a sense of wonder induces a feeling of loving kindness, increases our perceived sense of time (so we don't feel rushed), and makes us more generous. Even brief moments exposed to awe-inspir-ing scenery cause us to become more focused, less distracted, and more productive over the course of our day.

Here's an example from my editor, Margarita:

"One year when I was teaching sixth grade, a gift the students had given me, a goldfish they called Dr. Who, died. The kids were all sad, of course, and we buried Dr. Who outside in our class garden. Many months later, a boy, David, came running in at lunch. He grabbed me by the hand and hauled me out the back door without explanation. Stopping beside the first rose bloom of the year, David stabbed a finger at the flower and yelled, "Dr. Who regenerated!" I can't see a rose now, or hear the word wonder, without thinking of that beautiful moment."

People who experience high degrees of wonder are healthier and have better relationships. Social psychologists Dacher Keltner and Jonathan Haidt, who have studied the intersection of awe with compassion, morality, love, and meaning, feel there are five ways in which wonder can affect our daily life.

1. **Improve our relationship with time**
2. **Inspire our creativity**
3. **Give us hope and help us to appreciate life**
4. **Connect us to nature**
5. **Promote personal transformation**

Regardless of which strategies you choose, whether from above or by making up your own, make happiness your first priority—your yardstick for success. By doing so, you'll develop a more functional definition of success, reduce your stress, and function more effectively in demanding times. Calm, happy, satisfied people alone can be the calm in the eye of the storm.

Important points from Chapter Three:

- Peak performers understand the value of happiness
- Our mental programming prevents us from seeing the futility of conditional happiness
- Release demands and expectations, upgrading them to preferences
- Gratitude is the best tool to quickly increase your happiness index
- Create a strategy to enhance your self-awareness to control negative thinking
- Explore the idea of "beginner's mind" and embrace the experience of awe

Try These Exercises For Chapter Three:

It's easy to say that happiness is a choice. But it's also easy to reject that notion, because if you're feeling frustrated, depressed, overwhelmed, or exhausted, you can't just say, *"I choose to be happy,"* and have your emotions magically change. In fact, when people say, *"Just cheer up,"* you're most likely reaction will be to want to slug them!

A better way of looking at it is to say that **happiness is a workout.** You need the acceptance that working out helps, the willingness to do that workout, and the strength to begin. And of course, the more you do it, the stronger you become.

Just saying *"I choose to be happy"* is as foolish as saying, *"I choose to be strong."* The words are just the beginning, the intention expressed. But there's work behind it. You need to gain the necessary strength to redirect your focus to a more positive perspective. You also need to adopt the philosophical stance that **happiness is one possible option** toward which you can strive, that there is no situation which comes with the demand for unhappiness.

Given all that, what are some specific, tangible actions you can take that might produce movement toward an ultimately happier stance?

Here are a few to try this week...
• The moment you feel frustration, notice what you believe needs to change to be happy. Immediately shift your attention from getting that thing to thinking differently. Try looking at the situation as if you were a standup comedian. What's funny about the situation if you were to tell it from the stage?

• Explore the possibility that happiness creates success much more than the other way around. Boom.

• If you feel empty or overwhelmed, look for one bright spot in your current circumstance and apply mental strength to prevent yourself from reengaging in negative feelings like self pity.

• Imagine what you'd feel if the demands and expectations you or others have placed on you were suddenly gone. Notice the feeling and try to hold onto it.

• Look for opportunities to express gratitude to at least three people each day.

Chapter Four:
Clean Up Your Act...
Outside and In

*"Impeccability begins with a single act that has to
be deliberate, precise, and sustained. If that act is
repeated long enough, one acquires a sense of unbending
intent which can be applied to anything else. If that
is accomplished, the road is clear. One thing will lead
to another until the warrior realizes his full potential."*

—Carlos Castaneda

Few people like discipline. It's hard, it takes work,
and it violates our human drive to do whatever we
want to do whenever we want to do it. We love freedom. We love knowing that we have the "power" to
choose our actions moment by moment. Talk to an
artist or other creative person and you're likely to hear
the argument that discipline, order, structure, and the
like are of little use.

"I need to be free to create—to follow the prompt-ings of my soul!"

Yet for every creative urge, every nod to the unfet-tered flow of heart energy, there must be an equal amount of mind energy. Or, to put it another way, for every action prompted by the right brain, there must be a foundation built to contain it by the left brain.

Creativity without structure, without consequence, or without foundation, becomes nothing. You can't paint a picture on a canvas that doesn't exist. You need something on which to apply your creative energy. Not to mention that having a degree of order frees up more time to be creative.

Everything needs a structure, however minimal it might be. And this becomes even clearer under pres-sure. Those amphipods living seven miles below the surface of the ocean need a reliable structure to exist under pressure, and so do we.

Without structure and order, we would not exist. Without a skeleton and cellular architecture, we'd be nothing more than a puddle on the floor. Yet, time and again, in an effort to proclaim their freedom, peo-ple ignore the fact that freedom would be meaning-less if they weren't being held up by something.

What is that something? At a very basic level, it's the anatomical structure of our bodies, an interconnected system of parts that work together in harmony.

And in the same way that our bodies have a struc-ture that must obey nature's laws, so do our minds, our families, and our societies. These are all systems, and all systems large and small function or malfunction to the extent that those laws are obeyed.

What are the underlying structural imperatives that supersede even our sense of personal freedom? Integ-rity, impeccability, responsibility, and accountability.

When we violate the urgency of those forces, as we often do, we suffer.

Forty years ago, Werner Erhard said, *"Without integrity, nothing works."* Integrity, being true to your word, is essential to your survival. Still, we violate our integrity constantly. When you say, *"I will not eat chocolate this week,"* and then you do eat some in the name of freedom, your integrity takes a hit, even if no one is around to see you indulging. Your word becomes less trustworthy. The issue is one of personal power. You may say: I'm free to change my mind, to eat the chocolate. And of course, you'd be right. But, you may consider asking: Am I free to NOT eat the chocolate? When that desire arises, am I free to maintain my integrity and be true to my word, or am I a powerless victim of my own urges? I want it; I must have it. Is that freedom? Is that power? No.

Each time we turn our backs on our word, our word becomes less powerful. Over time, if you're consistently unreliable about the things you proclaim are important to you, you begin to create doubt about the trustworthiness of what you say next. That might be the doubt of another, such as a loved one who's learned not to trust what you say, or a deep inner doubt, such as a vague awareness that just because you say you're going to start an exercise program, that doesn't mean you will.

And that lack of inner confidence has consequences. Your sense of adventure suffers. Your belief in yourself erodes.

Your excitement for a new way of being dissolves before your eyes, if it ever shows up to begin with. Your ability to handle pressure diminishes. And what does that do to your sense of freedom and creativity? If you don't build in structure and order, chances are you won't stay creative for long. Instead you'll continue to doubt yourself and erode your self-expression.

The same can be said of the other carriers of structure at the mind level. Impeccability, the impetus to conduct your affairs with precision and to strive for excellence, is as important as integrity. William Blake said, *"mechanical excellence is the vehicle for genius."* Without the desire for and practice of constant improvement, **mechanical excellence cannot be achieved.** While Thelonious Monk played some very unconventional melodies and broke lots of musical rules, he was able to do so only because he had the foundation of a master musician. When a clown comically falters on the tightrope, always a breath away from falling, you can be sure he's a master acrobat and knows exactly how to maintain his balance.

Such is the case for you. You have no chance of surviving a high-pressure situation without integrity and impeccability. You'll let yourself down, you'll let others down, or the whole system will come tumbling down.

Personal responsibility is yet another of the inviolable forces that you can either cultivate, and thrive, or ignore, and suffer. When faced with pressure, it's very easy to skirt responsibility, to blame others, or to duck out the back door. To be responsible, to show up as a leader who can be trusted, you need to be willing and able to bear the burdens of the moment, even going so far as to own up to those ways in which you might have fallen short. Things happen, and you can either react unconsciously and emotionally, or respond appropriately. Responsibility therefore may be called the ability to respond. This requires strength

While Thelonious Monk played some very unconventional melodies and broke lots of musical rules, he was able to do so only because he had the foundation of a master musician.

of mind, what Joseph Chilton Pearce called **muscular mindedness.** Only when you've exercised your mind the way you would any bodily muscle can you be strong enough to demonstrate responsibility. Responsibility means you're a pillar of inner strength, a rock onto which others can cling when the waves of life are pounding the shore. High-pressure performers have a quality that comes from being responsible, that communicates wordlessly: Lean on me.

A close relative of impeccability, integrity, and responsibility is accountability. Accountability is a quality that welcomes the consequences of your actions or inactions. I tell you I'll be there tomorrow at eight o'clock. Integrity demands I take steps to make that happen. Impeccability requires that I don't take any of those steps half-assed. Responsibility insists that I carry the importance of my agreement with me. And accountability dictates that I either show up or I deal willingly with the consequences. Say I miss the meeting. Even if it wasn't my fault, even if it happened because of circumstances beyond my control, when I reach out to you, I apologize, I take responsibility, and I gladly offer up ways to make it up to you. By doing so, I take the burden off you, minimize your pressure, and contribute to a solution. One of the most important things you can do in high-pressure situations is to not be the cause of more pressure!

...all wisdom and ultimately enlightenment, must start with basic goodness.

Perhaps this should go without saying, but another element of cleaning up your act is taking a fearless inventory of your own morality. Buddhist teachings suggest that all spiritual attainment, all wisdom and ultimate enlightenment, must start with basic goodness. If you're not acting honorably in some way—if you're lying, cheating, stealing, or causing harm to another—you will be incapable of developing the focused concentration necessary to ultimately experience wisdom. Some part of you will resist inner growth as long as you're violating the basic tenets of goodness.

This can be a hard reality to accept in high-pressure situations. When you're moving fast, trying to accomplish a lot in the face of elevated expectations and tense emotions, you're apt to cut corners. When you're suffering through a lack of something, such as not having enough money, you might find ways of justifying little white lies that increase your chances of getting what you want or need. But this strategy is flawed and, like all the structural imperatives we've discussed, you violate it at your own peril. Sooner or later, all deceit catches up with you. So, treat morality not as a matter of right and wrong but as a matter of natural law. Like gravity, if you violate it, you will suffer, and not because you're bad, but because that is how natural laws work.

Here is a list of ideas to clean up your act and operate from a structure of integrity and goodness.

1. Make your bed.
Create order in your environment and a series of structured activities, beginning the moment you wake up, that will help you maintain that order. When you start your day with order, you'll remain more orderly throughout the day. When faced with the need to perform at your best under pressure, the precision of mind that comes from the habit of order will enhance your judgement and decrease your doubt. And with less clutter and disarray around you, your mind will be free to consider your options and invent solutions

more effectively.

2. Sharpen your sword.
Whenever you're not in the midst of using one of your tools, whether it be physical or mental, do what you can to improve that tool. Drill your action steps so they're automatic and second nature to you. Clean up your workspace so no amount of disorder might slow your response time. Get your physical needs met so you're at your best when you need to be. And of course, if your work involves the use of literal tools (or even swords), keep them in good shape. Be impeccable!

3. Create a ritual.
Discipline is a value unto itself and becomes more valuable when you're under pressure. Often it matters less what the discipline is than just the fact that you've got one. So, you can actually increase your effectiveness in high-pressure situations by making up something that you do at a certain time or under certain circumstances, and repeating it daily. One student found himself growing in strength of character and judgment after spending a month waking up an hour before he needed to and dropping a pebble out his window. Again, it doesn't matter what it is or how meaningless the action; all that matters is that you discipline yourself to follow that ritual.

4. Use a day planner.
Very few people have so well-developed a left brain that they can reliably keep their tasks and appointments in order without an external device like a day planner. Whether you write your action steps and goals into a physical book or put them into a calendar program on your computer, it's vital that you commit them to a written form. Until you do, either

you'll miss meetings and disappoint yourself and others or you'll waste valuable mental energy that could be used mastering your high-pressure situation. Create order on paper so you can free your mind to be more creative and resourceful.

5. Chunk down your goals.

In my Procrastination Annihilation home study course, I emphasize the importance of turning your goals and objectives into bite-sized pieces and knocking them off one by one. It's too easy to ignore or resist a big goal. Its enormity is its demise. You see a goal before you, realize it's too big to complete all at once, and you naturally shy away from it. By using your day planner and assigning small steps toward the completion of your goals to specific time slots, you're more likely to take action when the time comes to address one of those steps. And then, if you find yourself resisting a single step, you get to evaluate it to see if it's still too big or if there's something else in the way. The point is, small, manageable bites, judiciously built into your schedule, will maximize the chance that you'll get things done, which goes a long way toward relieving the pressure of your high-pressure life!

6. Check off your completions.

One of the inevitable realities of human nature is our thirst for acknowledgment. We love being appreciated and rewarded for our actions. When we accomplish something and there is nothing to mark or honor that accomplishment, we feel a subtle but real letdown. We become less likely to take action in the future. On the other hand, when we acknowledge and celebrate an accomplishment, we increase the likelihood that we'll accomplish more. An action rewarded is an action repeated. The simplest way to mark your accomplishments is to put a checkmark or V for victory next to the entry in your day planner. As you review days and weeks gone by and find evidence of your completions, you'll feel more confident and encouraged to continue taking action. This is particularly valuable in high-pressure situations. Since every step pales in comparison to the looming task before us, we're unlikely to mark our completions. But, if you acknowledge the small wins, you'll feel more energy to stay in the game for the big ones.

7. Close your loops.

My friend John, an ER nurse (a high-pressure job if ever there was one), recently used the term "closed loop communication" to describe what I had previously tried to explain to someone else in many more words. I was thrilled to have a term to expedite my explanation. Closing loops in communication means being responsible to get back to people with answers or just to let them know you got their message. It minimizes misunderstanding, prevents hurt feelings or incorrect assumptions, and maximizes safety. You tell me to get the bandages, wash out the wound, and wrap the arm. I hear "wash the bandages and wrap the wound." I don't repeat what I think I heard to you, so you never get to find out that I missed the message, and I end up doing something potentially dangerous. Even in a less intense situation, this is important. You call me to tell me something you think is important. I don't answer or respond to your message. You spend days thinking up all sorts of reasons I'm ignoring you, perhaps suffering over it. It turns out I was too busy to have the conversation, but I still could have prevented your misery by calling and completing the loop with a simple explanation.

"Got your message. No time to talk right now. I'll try you Tuesday." Make a commitment to respond to all communications even if your response can only be brief. Check your assumptions, and repeat back what you hear. In that way, all your communications are two-way, checked, acknowledged, and complete. High-pressure situations can't afford misunderstanding. And again, the best thing you can do in a high-pressure situation is to not add more pressure!

8. Empty your inbox.

Just as making your bed creates order in your physical world, emptying your inbox creates order in your virtual world. If you have dozens, hundreds, or even thousands of unanswered emails clogging up your inbox, each new addition is at best an annoyance and at worst a certainty to be ignored. If you think of your capacity to withstand pressure as being like a glass of water, having a full inbox is like starting off with your glass almost full. Any additional input spills over the top and makes a mess. You're less able to respond to your upcoming challenges when you're already near full. High-performing people in high-pressure positions understand the importance of mental space and the relationship between the physical and the mental. The more items in front of you, the less capacity you have for handling new input. Besides, that next email you get but don't respond to because you're already too far behind might be of vital importance. Clean out your inbox and be ready to receive whatever comes your way.

9. Write your code of conduct.

In cultivating basic goodness and a firm hold on morality, you can always turn to religion. The rules of behavior are easy to find there. But you're even more likely to adhere to a moral code if it's yours. Hopefully what you come up with won't differ substantially from the status quo, but still it's worth taking some time to write your own version of the Ten Commandments. Maybe you'll only have nine. Maybe you'll come up with a few new ones. Thou shalt not eat pizza on Tuesdays. Whatever you come up with is your code of conduct. As long as it includes the basic precepts of living honorably and doing no harm, you're probably on the right track. And, if you've written your code and carry it with you, it becomes a credo that informs every area of your life. When the pressure is on, you'll know how to behave despite the lure of the moment. Reflect on your personal morality, write your code, and live by it.

10. Embrace your apologies.

Most of us hate being wrong and hate being seen being wrong even more. As a result, we don't like apologizing. It's an acknowledgment that we were wrong, that we hurt someone, or that we let someone down. And we hate that. So, we get defensive, deny our responsibility, dodge the consequences, and maybe even avoid those we've wronged. This kind of immaturity works in direct opposition to the requirements of high pressure. Carrying the burden of having done something worthy of an apology and compounding it with denial or resistance creates a barrier to your own self-worth and between you and the other party. Ultimately, handling pressure is a team effort, and if you've burned bridges by avoiding admissions of wrongdoing, your team is not going to be there for you very long. Nor will you be there for yourself, since every time you violate the imperative of accountability, you lose a little bit of your honor. Realize that it's only the ego that resists showing vulnerability because it believes that being wrong makes you bad or unworthy. People who handle stress need to have the self-esteem to carry the burden of a mistake. They need to be able to acknowledge what they did, make it right, and move on. Don't try to protect yourself by having to be right. Let it be OK to be wrong, don't let it mean anything about your worth, and enjoy the goodwill you create with your colleagues when they know you're willing to own up to your mistakes. In fact, make every apology a personal celebration of your victory over small-mindedness.

11. Honor your word.

This can be very difficult if you're used to agreeing to things without much thought. If you're the kind of person who tells people you'll call them tomorrow and then don't write it down, chances are you don't put a lot of stock in what you say ... and neither does anyone else. If you're telling people you'll do something and you don't follow through, they know that about you. They may not say it, but they don't trust you. Starting now, whenever you make an agreement, however casual it might seem, write it down and commit yourself to following through. Once you start doing that, it will also become clear if you're the kind of person who overcommits yourself—saying yes when you should say no. If you have come to realize that about yourself, start considering before you answer a request. If there's any chance you can't do what's being asked of you, admit that. Tell the person you'd love to but you don't have time. Or make a counter-proposal, meaning, tell them what else you might be able to do instead. Or if it's a definite maybe, say that, too. It's OK to tell someone that you may or may not be able to do something. They can then tell you if they require a firm answer. If they do and you're not sure, say no. You're far better off saying no and disappointing them than saying yes and betraying them. You'll also notice that as you practice honoring your word, those things you commit to accomplishing will be much more likely to get done. When your word is trustworthy, it has power—and that's gold in a high-pressure situation.

12. List your distractions.
One of the biggest obstacles to peak performance is a mind filled with distractions. The unfinished business from your home projects, the fight you had with your partner, the financial worries you're carrying, and even the simple things like birthdays and vacations and Facebook posts all take their toll on your efficiency. When you arrive on the scene of your high-pressure job, the first thing you need to do is make a list of all the potential distractions floating around in your head. Once you've committed them to paper, you can forget them and put your entire focus on the job at hand. In the next chapter, we'll talk a lot about the power of focus, but for now, add this simple step to your day and you'll be more efficient and display better judgment in the midst of pressure and stress.

13. Be flexible.
All of the tools described above to increase your efficiency, organization, and integrity are wonderful aids. But they don't always account for what happens moment by moment. There will be times when your

best-laid plans become obsolete in the face of new information or a sudden crisis. While structure and a plan are great, it does you no good to doggedly hang on to them when they're no longer applicable or to lament the fact that things have changed just when you finally had a plan. Be willing to scrap your plan and make a new one with grace and humor. Let yourself be flexible not only in terms of your actions but also your attitudes. Learn to enjoy the uncertainty, the changes, the setbacks, and the confusion. If you can become the smiling face of relaxed acceptance in the midst of the latest monkey wrench, you'll not only feel better yourself, you'll also be a source of comfort to those around you.

The lessons in this chapter are perhaps the hardest to accept and embrace.

I've tried to give you a new way of seeing structure, order, integrity, morality, and the like. These are all qualities that we resist. but I have come to realize that a dose of structure and a code of conduct are worth the price of admission to the game of life. Take the time to address these areas, if nothing else than as an experiment, and see if you don't find what I've found: that discipline is freedom. The more you hold yourself to a high standard, the less you're buffeted by the forces of frustration or the pain of being overwhelmed. Clean up your act, not with the attitude of a petulant child being told what to do by your mother, but with the attitude of a warrior who knows the value of impeccability and relishes the rewards that come from victory.

Important points from Chapter Four:

- Discipline is freedom. Without order and structure, freedom doesn't exist
- The four structural imperatives are integrity, impeccability, responsibility, and accountability
- A moral code of conduct is a prerequisite to the next step on your path
- Build a strategy for greater order in your virtual and physical world
- Commit yourself to increasing your integrity and accountability by honoring your word

Try These Exercises For Chapter Four:

We have no idea just how incredibly indulgent we've become with ourselves. As a general rule, we are undisciplined, unreliable, and driven by our emotions. If we wake up tired, we move slowly, leave a trail of bedding on our way to the bathroom, miss a few teeth with our brush, and give ourselves the luxury of being grumpy with anyone who gets in our way.

Then, if we're challenged by a lack of time or money, we cut corners, give less, charge more, and allow ourselves to put our ethical foundation aside to expedite a return to normalcy.

How would our lives differ if we always gave 100%, treated others with respect despite our mood, returned all our calls, and honored every commitment?

We like this idea in theory, but we seldom recognize that the habit of integrity requires repetition and practice.

Here are a few things you can use to practice this week...

• Make your bed as soon as you rise each morning. **Do it well, with precision.**

• Eat more slowly and **gauge your hunger to know when to stop,** rather than clearing your plate

• Choose in advance **the way you'll react to unwanted situations** and then do so despite how you feel in the moment

• Pick **one meaningless action** and perform it on a regular schedule. For example, every evening at 6pm, throw a pebble out your bedroom window.

• Most importantly, become aware of your reactions to each of these activities. Do they feel like an imposition? **Do they seem foolish?** Do you feel resentful? Or, are you beginning to see the value of **structure as the week progresses?** Do you feel resentful? Or, are you beginning to see the value of structure as the week progresses?

Chapter Five:
Sharpen Your Focus

"The world is full of magical things patiently waiting for our senses to grow sharper."

—W.B. Yeats

Let's review our strategy so far. We're building an edifice one story at a time. The blueprint is happiness. It permeates the entire construction process. The basement is integrity. Without a strong foundation of honor, anything you build is doomed to collapse. And now, we're getting ready to build the first floor, which is focus.

Let me ask you something. What makes your job stressful? Would you describe it as a high-pressure job? Are you an ER nurse with a constant flow of crises to manage? Are you an officer of the law required to put yourself in harm's way? Are you a CEO charged with making high-consequence decisions that potentially affect the future of your company or the fate of your employees? Are you a teacher being held accountable for the success of your students, when so much of their performance is determined by home issues out of your control? Do you work in a company whose culture is toxic, surrounded by unhappy, demanding, or even hostile people? Are you in sales? Must you sell or die? Is your job security tied to your performance, your position at risk of being lost to other ambitious competitors?

Whatever your particular brand of high pressure, there are certain things you have in common with everyone else facing professional or even personal stress.

1. First, since this doesn't get said enough, you're awesome! If you're in a high-pressure situation, you've arrived there because of something special you possess. Maybe you're a very loving person and have chosen a career in which you're helping others, sometimes to your own detriment. Maybe you're a very honorable person, and you feel a personal sense of duty to teach or guide or hold others to a higher standard, even when they don't want to be held there. Maybe you're a visionary; you've taken on a high-pressure job to lead others and bring about positive change, often in the face of detractors and saboteurs. Maybe you're a savior, and you've dedicated your life to protecting and serving the needs of others in crisis, even when it means putting yourself in jeopardy. Or maybe you're a great provider; you've sacrificed your own comfort to make sure your family is well provided for, even when they don't appreciate it. Whatever it is for you, take a moment and acknowledge yourself for your courage, your perseverance, your compassion, your generosity, and your vision.

2. The second thing you have in common with all high- pressure dwellers is the desire to learn, grow, and improve. You wouldn't be reading this book if you didn't want to discover new tools and perspectives that might increase your effectiveness.

3. Third, the stress you feel is not the result of what you're doing so much as what you're thinking and feeling about what you're doing. If you had more control over your thoughts and feelings, you'd experience less stress in your current situation.

Which brings us to the fourth commonality among all high-pressure dwellers.

4. You have an untapped resource for making your job much easier and less stressful, to control your thoughts and emotions and achieve balance. This is the key to becoming the calm spot in the eye of the storm.

That resource is focus.

Let me explain. Focus is the ability to direct your attention to one place to the exclusion of all other input, and to do so from a neutral stance—nonjudgmentally.

Increased focus comes with many benefits:

Listening

People with the capacity to focus their attention despite distractions and frustrations are better listeners. If your mind isn't preoccupied by an endless tape loop of thought, you can bring a greater percentage of your attention to the person addressing you, which increases cooperation. Studies show that people feel more valued by those who demonstrate good listening skills. **That means your colleagues, co-workers, managers, and team members will appreciate you more, feel better in your presence, and most likely share more fully with you than they would with someone displaying divid-**

ed attention. In high-pressure situations, you need to rely both on the cooperation and the good-will of your team members. Becoming a better listener goes a long way toward promoting both.

Your ability to listen also creates a climate that promotes greater self-esteem and self-expression among those to whom you're speaking. It's been said that we talk into other people's listening. This means our ability to communicate, and sometimes even to think clearly, hinges on the degree to which we're being given attention. Have you ever noticed that when people you're talking to aren't paying attention you find it more difficult to formulate a thought?

In high-pressure situations, information is vital. Lacking important data can be the difference between a successful outcome and an unmitigated disaster. Listening promotes the flow of information.

Finally, when people feel heard, it increases their sense of self-respect, and they rise to the occasion. When they feel better about themselves, they're more likely to engage with you in a problem and offer viable solutions.

Solving

Another benefit of heightened focus is the ability to spot solutions and opportunities that most people walk right past. Our minds are habituated to our environments. Once we've been in a place long enough, our minds start taking shortcuts and "going blind" to information, data, and other components of our surroundings. Have you ever noticed a picture on somebody's desk and asked if it was new, only to be told it has been sitting there for months?

This tendency to go blind to your surroundings is a valuable mental shortcut, to minimize extraneous data and prevent you from overloading your circuits. But in times of crisis, change, or stress, many of the things you've been conveniently ignoring might hold the key to your salvation. So at high-pressure times, it's important to be able to bring your environment back into focus.

Accuracy

Another reason focus is so important is the obvious one: we make fewer mistakes. We all like to believe that we only need a tiny bit of our attention to navigate masterfully through any situation. Yet research shows otherwise. Nobody likes to believe, for example, that they're incapable of texting or talking on the phone while driving without sacrificing safety. We know that's true; the traffic safety data is irrefutable. But we're stubborn and proud. We refuse to believe or act as if we understand the truth that dividing our focus inevitably minimizes our effectiveness.

Efficiency

Focus also increases efficiency. Whether you're triaging patients or advancing on an enemy or working on a project, the degree to which you can narrow your focus to the one thing you're doing determines how quickly and accurately you'll do it. Multitasking, though tempting, has nowhere near the track record of hyper-focus. This is why it's so important to prioritize, an activity that starts before you enter the pressure cooker. You need a system of action and a protocol that will help you know what to do and in what order. Otherwise, your attention will be scattered to the wind when things go awry.

Toughness

Focus makes you more resilient, more capable of withstanding crisis and change. When you can deliberately select where to put your attention, you're less likely to be thrown off-course by the emotional reactions that occur when unexpected or overwhelming things start happening.

Relief

Focus is an escape valve. In stressful jobs, sometimes the pressure is relentless. It's literally impossible to maintain peak performance without mental breaks. Our nervous systems and hormonal systems aren't designed for consistent stress, but rather for bouts of intensity followed by periods of recovery. As life has become more complex and jobs have become more demanding, we're more likely to find ourselves in situations where the challenges never stop. Although they may not stop, you must. Our stubborn minds seldom give us permission to pause, thinking that any break in the relentless pursuit of a goal will only slow its ultimate completion. But that's not true. All evidence points to the importance of periodic breaks.

But we must understand what a break is. If you stop doing something but don't stop thinking about it, that's not a break. You need to shut it off completely and trust the fact that, not only will your problem be waiting for you when you re-engage, you'll be more resourceful for having paused.

The power to stop thinking about something when the inertia of that thought is intense comes from focus. The more you develop your power of focus, the more reliably you can turn your attention away from whatever is vying for it and replenish your mind.

Wisdom

Of all the benefits of focus, the most powerful, important and misunderstood is its ability to promote wisdom.

Wisdom is a higher order of mental function. Wisdom supersedes knowledge. It's one thing to know what to do; it's another thing to know when to do it or why not to do it. Wisdom is judgment, understanding, compassion, patience, and respect all rolled into one.

Perhaps wisdom is hard to define, but chances are you know it when you see it. You know people who have it and others who don't, and you'd rather be with those who have it. That's because a wise person is trustworthy. They see the forest for the trees. They have vision and are capable of predicting how things are likely to go. They honor Truth. They understand the interconnectedness of things, so they're unlikely to take actions for short-term gain, ignorant of the long-term consequences.

The wise are not reactive, because they've achieved an inner knowing that all situations are inherently fluid.

And they're generally calm. They're not reactive, because they've achieved an inner knowing that all situations are inherently fluid. All things change, and there's no point in clinging to what is or lamenting what once was. The wise are unattached. They take actions that produce the best results given their understanding of the situation, but they don't become insistent on the outcome. They recognize themselves as one player on the field with only limited power to produce the end result. The forces of nature, the opposing party, and perhaps God, all have a say in the outcome. So while victory is worth striving for, surrender is sometimes inevitable, especially if it means living to fight another day.

Armed with the wisdom-induced willingness to back away from our battle plan, we can think on our feet and create new strategies on the fly. Those who are attached to an outcome are also often attached to the method they've selected for achieving it. And they're unwilling to consider a change of plans. Like the monkey trap—a box with a small hole and a banana inside that a hungry monkey grabs through the hole, but then can't extract because the grasping fist is bigger than the hole—we cling to our solutions while better ones are presenting themselves all around us. The wise can let go of the banana to reach out for something better.

How does focus create wisdom? To answer that question, we need to consider where wisdom comes from. While we know that knowledge comes from study and experience, we're not as clear on the source of our wisdom. Ancient philosophers and spiritual teachers tell us that our wisdom is innate. It bubbles up from deep within. It's what some call our source energy. Others describe it as God within. Regardless of how you frame it or name it, it's worth embracing the idea that your wisdom is the deepest and most profoundly real part of who you are.

Surrounding your deep source of wisdom are layers of habitual thought, personality, preferences, and beliefs. Some of those layers are functional. Others not so much. While you might believe yourself to be smart or dumb, attractive or hideous, capable or incapable, each of these is a conclusion reached by your mind, which in itself is a construct of your experience: what your parents taught you, what you came to believe based on how you were treated by the kids in your neighborhood, what your culture has dictated to be true and false, and all the other millions of pieces of data that you've spun together into the layers of your personality.

And beneath all that is an inner knowing, which is wisdom itself. That part of you, your source energy, knows your limitless capability for growth, knowledge, and love. The path to wisdom is the gradual re-identification of yourself, not as your mind but as that deep, infinitely perfect being you really are, beneath all the layers of mental content. You are not your thoughts.

And this is where it gets very interesting. If your layers of personality, preferences, beliefs, and worldview are held in place by and characterized by thought, an incessant yet unnoticed tape loop draining your power 24-7, what characterizes the deeper source energy, the place from which your wisdom flows?

Silence.

It is from a place of silence that all great ideas arise. It was silence that bore the great scientific discoveries of Isaac Newton, Niels Bohr, and Albert Einstein. It was silence that cultivated the creativity of Leonardo da Vinci, Vincent Van Gogh, and Andy Warhol. And it's silence that gives rise to your most brilliant and transformational strategies. In times of stress, your ability to achieve silence is directly tied to your ability to achieve wisdom ... and find solutions.

Practically speaking, those who practice silence through meditation have discovered that finding a quiet place within gives rise to a powerful recognition upon which all wisdom is based: a recognition that all things are impermanent.

The practice of silence gives rise to a new identity within yourself.

Everything that is, was, or will be is temporary in nature. All your troubling thoughts are temporary. Left alone, they are destined to dissipate. All your emotions, no matter how painful, are temporary. Left alone, they, too, will vanish. Likewise, all the challenges, crises, and aggravations you face are temporary. They have no inherent permanence. Eventually, they, like your thoughts, your emotions, and even you yourself, will disappear.

For the unwise, that's reason for panic. We cling to everything, including life itself. Yet the wise accept the impermanent nature of reality and embrace the now. What's happening right now? What can I do to appreciate this moment? How can I make this situation better now?

The practice of silence gives rise to a new identity within yourself. You begin to cultivate a part of your mind called the witness. This is nothing mystical or magical. It's simply the result of practicing the discipline of stepping out of your stream of thought long enough to watch yourself thinking; to separate yourself from the whirring of your mind. You're in the midst of your challenges, but you're simultaneously witnessing them and witnessing yourself dealing with them. You're unemotionally observing your emotions, detached and free of suffering.

On the inside, this feels like a great relief. Suddenly you're not suffering over your suffering. Gradually, you're not ruminating over your challenges. You're just meeting them quietly and with wisdom.

On the outside, you seem calm, quiet, and capable—because indeed you are. Your focus has led you to a state of mind that, rather than fighting with change, embraces it, allows it, dances with it, and artfully transforms it. Think about the greatest leaders you've ever known or heard about. They're almost always the quietest ones in the room! This is the true essence of power.

The wisdom brought about by focus can be equated to the sudden recognition that the life-or-death struggle in which you thought you were embroiled was just a game—as if you suddenly woke up and realized you were playing Monopoly, not losing your house.

Although it's in our nature to worry and panic and catastrophize, it's worth realizing that this tendency is a leftover remnant of our ancestry. Our nervous systems are wired to release neurohormones for the fight-or-flight response, in order to save us from being eaten by a saber-tooth tiger. In our modern world, that reaction we feel when someone gives us a dirty look is just an artifact, an overreaction based on our neurological heritage. If you're wise, you won't buy into it, even when it feels real. Most of the time, when you perceive a threat, it's an illusion.

Some people fear that if they become unattached they'll lose their edge and no longer have the will to win. But think about a game. You still play to win, yet there's something fundamentally good about the game, whether you do or not. It's the thrill of the chase.

Thriving in high-pressure situations requires the same attitude.

Those who excel in times of crisis maintain some degree of proportion; otherwise, they collapse into their emotions. Staying centered and calm demands an ability to handle your more intense situations as if they were a game. And that takes focus. Focus lets you catch yourself being pulled into unnecessary drama. It reminds you that nothing is really that dire. And it allows you the emotional distance to make intelligent choices.

Hopefully I've made a compelling case for focus. And indeed, those who achieve a measure of focus will happily tell you its value. But there are a few obstacles we face when it comes to focus.

The first is that focus is hard. It's a lot easier to get pulled into your life drama than to stay calm and centered and direct your mind to the most useful strategy in the moment.

This is the reason pilots are taught to "fly the instruments" rather than flying "by the seat of their pants." When I studied for my pilot's license, I spent many hours drilling on the habit of consulting my instruments to determine my position in space. Here's why.

Let's say you're flying through a cloud and can't

see anything out the window. If the instruments say you're descending, you're descending. You need to respond to that data and level off. This may be in direct opposition to what your body, the seat of your pants, is telling you. You may feel like you're climbing when you're descending. **The combination of movements through space can easily give you false data in your body.** For example, if you're descending and simultaneously turning, you'll feel pressure on your seat that feels like you're climbing. If you respond to that input instead of what your instruments tell you, you're likely to compound the problem and fall out of the sky. But to learn to trust your instruments over your body is a learning process, one you fight all the way. It takes a few or more repetitions of seeing that you're wrong before you'll let go of your sense of being right.

It's like that with focus. Your mind will demand that you handle difficult situations based on what feels right, even if that response actually compounds your problem. So, you need to drill the more functional response. When X happens, I do Y. I may not feel like it or believe it will work, but that's what my training tells me to do. My focus remains on the appropriate trained response, not on the distraction of what I feel.

Another reason we resist learning to focus is that it's an evasive state. More often than not, even the most unconscious people think they're already focused. That's because when you're not focused, you're not present. And if you're not present, who's left to tell you that you're not focused? It's only when your mind returns from wandering that you become aware of yourself, and in that moment you are focused. So, you never get to see yourself not being focused. It's like the light in your refrigerator. Whenever you open the door, it's on. As soon as you close the door, presumably it goes off. But how do you know?

Focus is finite.
You only have so much to go around before you need to defocus. That's why breaks are so important. If you attempt to maintain focus for longer than is healthy, you'll eventually start making mistakes, losing your temper, and becoming less efficient. You need to honor the ebb and flow of your attention.

Focus is trainable.
Like a muscle, the more you exercise it, the stronger it grows. As you begin to develop the practice of exercising your focus muscles, all the benefits above will become clearer, and you'll have more stamina to maintain focus between needed breaks.

Focus is fragile.
It often leaves us just when we need it most; our attention wanders off into non-vital areas, sometimes just for fun. Our mental habit of resting in the past and the future is a seductive trap. Not that there's anything wrong with remembering or fantasizing, but it's imperative to be able to bring yourself back to the moment, especially when demand is high.

With focus being so important and with human nature being so stubborn, how do we develop the power of focus in order to strengthen our capacity for calm in the face of pressure? There are many tools for this purpose; here we'll focus on three.

Strategy #1:

The first tool is practicing meditation. Of all the methods for learning to focus and achieve silence, none is more powerful or better researched than mindfulness meditation. As a daily practice, meditation has the proven benefits of diminishing unwanted mental chatter, calming your nervous system, and making you smarter. In fact, in several studies, it was shown that meditation increases the thickness of vital parts of your cerebral cortex, the thinking part of your brain.

Seasoned meditators have lower levels of cortisol and epinephrine, the stress-inducing hormones, and higher levels of oxytocin, dopamine, and serotonin, the hormones that evoke feelings of happiness, relaxation, and love.

When you meditate, you change your relationship with your feelings in such a way that you don't get upset when an unpleasant sensation arises, but rather get curious and compassionate.

After you've been at it a while, meditation will rewire your brain so the parts that register painful feelings communicate more directly with the assessment centers than with the personal centers of your cerebral cortex, meaning that you'll take things less personally and default to simply finding solutions.

As your brain increases its processing power, it's able to stay a step ahead of the circumstances arising around you, and you'll feel an interesting shift in the way you experience them, as if you're able to see problems coming a mile away. It's like those Matrix movies, where the bullets seem to go slow enough for the character to get out of the way. That shift also applies to how you experience your own emotions.

Instead of being overtaken by them, you'll feel them arising slowly and you'll be able to parry them before they take hold.

Another powerful result of meditation is compassion. If you're in a helping profession, you know it's not uncommon to feel drained by your own empathy for someone in pain. Compassion is empathy plus detachment. You still care, but it won't burn you out because that caring will exist within the context of love and acceptance rather than fear and rejection. Compassion, therefore, makes you a better healer and helper.

These benefits and more are the reason peak performers in sports, medicine, and business all practice meditation. The US military is now making mindfulness meditation part of its basic training. Doctors are now using it before surgery to minimize errors. And all those Chicago Bulls and LA Lakers championships were won by Phil Jackson, the coach who introduced meditation to sports superstars such as Michael Jordan.

The bottom line is that if you want to perform better with less stress, meditation is the way to go.

If you don't already have a practice of your own, here's a simple, direct approach to meditation that requires no belief, no dogma, no religion, and no mumbo jumbo.

Do this with sincerity, and within days, you'll begin to notice a shift in your mental state. Your stress will diminish, your sense of humor will sharpen, and you'll make better decisions during high-pressure times. In fact, as your focus increases from this practice, you'll find everything requires far less effort.

Twelve steps for a simple meditation practice:

1. Sit comfortably in an upright position with your back straight, arms comfortably in your lap.
2. Keep your eyes and your mouth closed.
3. Take three *"cleansing breaths,"* forgetting your cares.
4. Commit to using this time for self-inquiry, not thought.
5. Focus on your breath as it enters and leaves your nostrils.
6. Don't try to change anything you notice. Accept it as it is.
7. Give yourself a brief reminder to maintain perfect awareness and acceptance.
8. Begin to become aware of the sensations over your body. Move your attention up and down your body, uncritically noticing whatever feelings arise.
9. If you become bored, distracted, frustrated, or overwhelmed, realize that these, too, are just sensations. Observe them as you would all other sensations or thoughts.
10. Practice for at least twenty minutes. Do as much as an hour at a time. It's best to practice both in the morning and in the evening.
11. Use this same practice any time something upsetting or stressful occurs during your day. Bring your attention, as quickly as possible, into your body and away from your thoughts.
12. Remind yourself that you are not your thoughts; you are not your mind.

As you practice the art of simple observation, a very interesting thing will begin to happen. When situations arise in your life that used to cause you to react negatively, you'll find yourself more and more quickly leaving behind the churning of your mind—the part that says, "This shouldn't be!"—and directing your attention with curiosity and wonder to your inner sensations. Freed of the emotional impact, you'll find it much easier to refocus on the problem at hand.

Strategy #2:

The second strategy for sharpening your focus is simply to take time to notice the beauty around you. Take a walk in nature, look at beautiful pictures, stare at a fire, sit by a lake. Even try to notice beauty in unconventional places. Practice playful perception so you can look at a slushy road as if you were hovering over the surface of a distant planet. Or look at things more closely than usual. Even a few minutes observing the fascinating texture of the wallpaper in your office can strengthen your focus. Research now shows that even brief exposure to awe-inspiring images (and with the right attitude and focus, what's not awe-inspiring?) increases our generosity, our patience, our endurance, and our sense of well-being.

Strategy #3:

The third strategy we'll discuss is to cherish the mundane. Consider the most menial, boring, repetitive tasks of your day, such as washing dishes, and commit to doing them with absolute focus. Try washing those dishes without talking, watching TV, or even thinking about anything else. Develop the discipline to tell yourself with each breath that washing that next dish is like bathing your cherished child. Sound ridiculous? Well, you'll break fewer dishes ... and when you make the mundane sacred, everything takes on a more sacred quality. How does this influence your ability to thrive in high-pressure situations? How could it not?

Regardless of what method or methods you choose, set an intention to practice strengthening your focus muscles. Take the time to discipline yourself through repeated mindful actions.

You might even notice that activities you previously found annoying or stressful take on a calming quality. For example, I remember I used to find it irritating to mentor students who came to shadow me in my chiropractic office. The incessant questions and such. Once I started my mindfulness practice, though, it became clear that having an inexperienced person with me forced me to think more critically, justify my actions more intelligently, and become more aware of how much I actually knew. Once you master your ability to focus, even the things that once annoyed you could become gifts.

So, quiet your mind and get out of your own way!

Important points from Chapter Five:
- Focus is vital to coping with stress
- The greatest gift of focus is wisdom
- Many obstacles exist to attaining focus
- Practice is necessary to develop focus
- Meditation, noticing beauty, cherishing the mundane and increased focus as the week progresses?

These Exercises For Chapter Five:

Take this week to shut off the news, Twitter, or any other news source. I'm serious. Give yourself a mental fast by not reading the news, or watching political debates, or war coorespondents. **If you must watch television,** start watching only comedies or uplifting documentaries, or concerts. Be present when you are watching. No crime dramas either.

If television is not your thing, **then pick up a good book.** Something uplifting—pick one of the books in the suggested reading appendix at the back of this book. The key is to guard your mind, and stop allowing outside influences to clutter up your thoughts.

Do this for an entire week. I know...you're probably thinking *"But Steve, how will I keep up with what's going on in the world?"* **Trust me. You'll survive without the news...and it will survive without you.**

At the end of the week, on the last day, do a technology blackout as well. Go dark for one full day.

Do your very best to be disciplined in this practice.

At the end of the week, write down the clarity you have gained, the peace of mind you are experiencing and the focus you have attained due to this exercise. Also, what projects have you finished? What did you do with your free time?

Start integrating this into your life as a once a week practice, or something you do monthly, or even a week long retreat once a year.

You deserve these moments of solitude... without distraction.

Chapter Six:
Lean Into The Pressure

"If you can keep your head when all about you are losing theirs ... you'll be a man, my son!"

—Rudyard Kipling
A Father's Advice To His Son

When I was eleven years old, I had a huge crush on my classmate, Susan Bodeck. I can say that now because I finally confessed it to her. As an insecure child, I didn't have the courage to speak up, and I was pretty sure I'd be rejected if I did. When I finally told her about it, sitting on the porch of her Long Island home after being reunited by Facebook forty years later, she asked me why I hadn't said anything when we were kids. Apparently, I might have had a shot!

Back then, I couldn't say anything, so instead I embarked on a very brief career as a stalker. One day, I rode my bicycle to the other end of town, crossing a couple of busy streets I probably shouldn't have been anywhere near, and stopped in front of her house, staring. Susan Bodeck was in there! It gave me almost the same thrill I got whenever I looked at the one-inch picture of her face I'd cut out of our class photo and taped secretly on the back of my closet door under the ties, where nobody would ever find it!

The thrill came to an abrupt end when her door swung open, and racing out in front of her was a gigantic, ferocious German shepherd. It charged my way with a look you wouldn't describe as welcoming. I turned and ran for my life. Bad move. The dog promptly reached me in my retreat and took a big chunk out of my right buttock cheek. It wasn't clear which was worse, the physical pain or the humiliation.

When I told my parents, the first thing they said (later to be repeated by everyone I ever told) was, *"Never run from a charging dog. You have to stand and face it."*

"Now you tell me!" I thought.

It was good advice, given too late—and who knows? If I'd done that, maybe my life would have taken a completely different turn.

It's like that with all the pains and pressures of life. If you run from them, they'll bite you in the butt.

You need to stand and face them, even lean into them.

In contrast to that scarring incident of yesteryear, here's a ferocious dog story with a happier ending. The day I first experienced mindfulness meditation, I was blown away by how it made me feel. Later that same day, I took a bike ride along the Burlington, Vermont, waterfront and along the way passed the spot where I'd been startled several times before by a seriously deranged, mouth-frothing, loudly barking pit bull who was prevented from eating me by only a one-foot gap between me and the extent of his lead.

Passing the spot that particular day I heard only the growling bark, more subdued than usual. I didn't see him because he didn't come up over the bank, and I wondered why. Getting off my bike, I looked down into his yard and found him crouched by the side of a fallen limb, around which his lead had become wrapped. He was stuck in place, and he looked miserable.

Without a thought, I walked down the bank, crouched by his side, and began to untangle him. His foaming mouth and ferocious bark, inches from my face, gradually subsided, to be replaced first by a look of suspicion, then confusion, and finally gratitude. And then ... he kissed me.

I gave him a pat, climbed the bank, hopped on my bike and pedaled on. It took me about a minute before it sank in. I had taken action with literally no concern for my own safety, out of pure compassion for his suffering. And he got it ... quicker than I had!

What I learned in that moment was that presence and fear cannot coexist.

What I learned in that moment was that presence and fear cannot coexist. When you're deeply present in the moment, you're moved by something much more profound than fear. Love becomes the dominant motivator.

How does that play out in high-stress situations? First, there's the inner transformation. When you begin to live in a state of presence, of deep focus on the now, your inner experience is calm and loving. You become willing to see beyond what's on the surface. Instead of seeing a growling monster, you see the wounded one in need.

Then there's the outer transformation. By seeing the real need and rising above your fear, you act with compassion. You do what needs to be done. You become a source of healing and support for others. What moments before might have seemed like an insurmountable problem caused by fundamentally bad people, your transformed state of consciousness allows you to see something more profound, to act in a more loving way, and to elevate that high-pressure situation to a vehicle for greater love. That's power!

But none of that would be possible if you were to continue to run from every charging dog. As long as you continue to avoid confrontation, stress, and discomfort, you'll never get to turn that beast into a lamb. You'll just keep getting bitten.

Leaning into your stress, into your pressure, and into your pain means being willing to feel something you've spent your life avoiding. **Standing firm in the face of discomfort, fear, doubt, and stress takes courage; it's not what you've been trained for.**

But the moment you decide to lean in, to not run, your capacity for thriving in difficult situations changes instantly.

Here's how:

First, you spot the impending challenge; you see the charging dog, the angry co-worker, the nerve-wracking presentation you've got to give—and you panic. Your heart races. Your instinct is to run.

But having spent the past several days practicing meditation, you know better than to react to an emotion. Instead, you watch it, notice it, embrace it.

It dissolves into nothing but energy in your body, and then it dissipates.

You're left with nothing but an open heart.

The dog is still charging, but somehow now in slow motion. It's no longer a threat. You smile your Superman smile, send out goodwill through your eyes, and the dog stops charging. The co-worker stops yelling. The important presentation loses its sense of doom. And you calmly do what needs to be done.

The process is simple. Whenever you notice a stress reaction in response to something happening around you, redirect your attention, your focus, to the feeling itself. Notice the sensation in your body, allow it, embrace it, breathe into it, and let it go. Return your attention to the issue at hand and notice how it's lost its charge.

As you master this technique, you'll find that you welcome what you used to think of as stressful situations, because each one is an opportunity to practice your new technique. And in so doing, you'll begin to see how few of the things you thought were dangerous, horrible, or unacceptable really are that way.

This process, along with your meditative and other focus practices, will give you greater and greater wisdom with each repetition. Ultimately, you'll find that you can let go of the things you once thought were essential to your happiness and, little by little, arrive in a place of calm acceptance. Eventually, you might see through the entire illusion.

If you've ever been to Disney's Hollywood Studios, chances are you stuck around for the evening show, a 3-D sound-and-light extravaganza projected onto a wall of water emanating from a huge fountain. The mist forms a surface on which movie images appear, the most dramatic being a scene from The Sorcerer's

Apprentice, starring Mickey Mouse. Those images can be scary; kids cry. But if you were to walk up to the fountain, you'd be able to walk right through the images. They're just an illusion, as insubstantial as the vapor upon which they're projected.

It's like that with our fears. They seem so big and scary, and we're averse to going anywhere near them. But when we muster enough courage and wisdom, we can walk right through them, and the journey is much shorter than we ever could have imagined.

Lean into your fear, your pressure, and your stress. Breathe, observe, smile, and walk on.

Look, let's face it. Given the choice, we'd always prefer to avoid unpleasant experiences. We hate pain. We hate pressure. We hate stress, not to mention demanding bosses, incompetent employees, jealous co-workers, endless aggravation, and irritating people. And so, naturally, we avoid them.

And not just physically. Sometimes we're right next to them and we're secretly a million miles away. Sometimes we can even be looking someone right in the eye and not hearing a word they say. We're very good at avoiding what we don't like.

But what I've offered you in this chapter is a new way of experiencing all that. Reverse the paradigm, so instead of making it your goal to avoid pain, make it your goal to gain freedom, which comes from letting go of the need to have things your way. Once you've done that, each painful experience is a new opportunity to help you with that challenge.

For example, if you annoy me, I think to myself:

Thank you! You've just shown me one more of my addictions that I can practice releasing. And I'll know I was successful when the time comes that I can look at you and that annoying thing you do, and feel nothing but love and compassion.

Remember, your stress is not about anyone or anything else but yourself. It's the result of the programmed, automatic, habitual, and often unconscious interpretations you're making about the situation. It's just an illusion, lights on a wall of vapor. Change the interpretation and you change your experience. Walk through the mist ...

And in the end, you're free.

Important points from Chapter Six:

- Don't run from your stress; it'll bite you... you know where
- Don't avoid what you don't like, even mentally
- Leaning in allows you to move through your resistance
- On the other side of stress is freedom
- The technique to move through involves observing your sensations

Try These Exercises For Chapter Six:

The process of leaning in to pain, discomfort, or emotional turmoil is counterintuitive. Everything in our upbringing tells us to run from pain or to fight it. As a result, we're locked into a cycle of self-preservation within which we seldom get to discover that our discomfort, whether physical or emotional, is temporary.

While we struggle to figure out what to do to bring our pain to an end, we do little more than intensify and prolong it, because the thoughts and strategies with which we occupy ourselves are like logs thrown onto a fire. As long as we continue adding fuel, the fire continues to burn.

How can we develop the strength and discipline to resist the thoughts that prolong our pain? How can we stop throwing logs on the fire?

Here are a few steps to change the mental habits of reacting and resisting...

• Purposely bring to mind something aggravating to you. Perhaps a recurring fight.

• Allow yourself to ruminate in the drama of that situation until you can feel the pain.

• Now stop thinking about the situation and instead turn your attention to the pain itself.

• Explore its location, quality, size, and character.

• Breathe into the pain; soften to it. Embrace it. Let it be OK to feel.

• Notice how it changes its quality and character over the time of this exercise.

• Notice how, after a few moments, your thinking about the underlying situation has changed.

Chapter Seven:
Assemble Your Lifeboats

*"Life is not a solo act. It's a huge collaboration, and
we all need to assemble around us the people who
care about us and support us in times of strife."*

—Tim Gunn

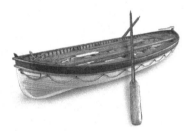

Earlier, I alluded to a concept called necessary
strength. If a major component of stress-free performance is the ability to focus—to keep one's attention from being drawn into habitual thought patterns
and instead keep it on the task at hand—it stands to
reason that your focus needs to be strong enough to
do that.

There's a constant tug-of-war going on between
your habitual mind and your most resourceful self;
between your constant inner dialogue and the
experience of silence. If you haven't developed the
strength of your "focus muscles," you'll inevitably be
drawn into negative self-talk, anxiety, distraction,
and the like. In turn, these mental activities will cause

stress and suffering.

That's the suffering you feel when you're in a high-pressure situation and believe it's the situation itself causing your stress. It's not. It's your lack of strength, your inability to turn off your brain. So, dis-empowering thoughts repeat themselves endlessly in your head, and you suffer.

The tools I've provided thus far are designed to strengthen your focus muscles, to give you power over the noise in your head. But, like physical ex-ercise, it takes time. The longer you meditate and practice mindfulness, the more power you'll gain to not get pulled down the rabbit hole.

But, in the meantime, life doesn't stop. You proba-bly don't have the time or inclination to sit in a cave until your mind gets strong enough to handle all the challenges to serenity that you face. So, what do you do?

You assemble your lifeboats. You make a plan in advance for what to do when it gets to be too much.

If you are too weak to swim across a particular body of water, but circumstances are such that you have no choice but to try, you'll be wise to station a lifeboat nearby into which you can climb when you start drowning. It's the same with high-stress situations. If you ha-ven't yet mastered the ability to be in stressful situations with-out losing your cool, you need something or someone to pull you out before you flounder in your emotions and drown in the stress.

Assembling your lifeboats means preparing for the eventual certainty that, at some point, you'll need to be saved from yourself.

Lifeboats come in two categories: people and systems.

Your people lifeboats are friends, but you need to choose them wisely. Not everyone in your life is equipped or willing to be a lifeboat. What you need at times when you're stressed and overwhelmed is someone who can give you the space to talk about your fears and frustrations but who won't buy into them. You don't need someone pouring more fuel onto your fire.

In fact, using that metaphor, imagine your aggravations as a fire. You can feel them burning inside you: the anger, the anxiety, the overwhelm. As you sit in front of the fire, you constantly think of all the reasons you feel the way you do; all the wrongs of your detractors, all the things you should have said or done, all the reasons your situation is bad and wrong, and all the ways you're right and deserving of more than this horrible feeling. Each of those thoughts is a log, and every time you think one, you throw another log on the fire. And so, it continues to burn, and you continue to suffer. Only when you finally stop throwing logs on the fire—that is, only when you return to silence—can the fire burn out and allow you to feel calm again.

Some of our friends are log-throwers. They'll sit by your side and burn along with you, even giving you more reasons that you're right. They'll say, "How awful! I can't believe she did that to you! She's such a ..." And, in so doing, those friends add fuel to your fire and reinforce your stance as a victim of someone or something outside yourself.

It may feel good, short term, but in the long run, this kind of "support" is damaging to you. It validates your sense of righteousness and entitlement, it disempowers you, and it puts more negative energy into the world.

What you ultimately want is for the fire to burn out. You want as quickly as possible to return to a state of inner peace and to rise above the notion of yourself as a victim.

We've already discussed the inner process to do this, which is to simply observe your feelings without thought or content until they begin to dissolve. When you're strong enough to do that, nothing is more powerful than this approach, because it returns you to your calm, loving center and reminds you that you are more than your thoughts. You then reconnect with wisdom, with source energy, and feel powerful again.

> **You want as quickly as possible to return to a state of inner peace and to rise above the notion of yourself as a victim.**

When you're not strong enough to do that, you need support, but not to keep you stuck in your lower mind state, however seductive it might seem. You need someone to see you as the powerful person you really are when you don't see it yourself.

So, what do you need from a supportive friend? Mostly silence. You want to find a friend who can beam love and acceptance at you as you throw your logs on the fire. In that way, you soon start to see yourself the way they see you, and you rise above your pain. This, in the truest sense, is healing.

Here's an example from Lysa, who lost her husband to cancer:

"After Tom died, a good friend in Los Alamos who had become a widow two years earlier allowed me short "pity-me parties" knowing they were essential to grieving and would move me on to the next

stage, because she had gone through the same experience.

When it comes to workplace stress, a good friend who is compassionate and knows that you're much more than the victim you're currently playing will smile and even laugh as you share your woes, like you're telling them a really funny story. They're not laughing at you but with you (they've been there, too!). You're just not laughing yet. Before long, though, you'll have no choice but to see the humor and let it go.

Being witnessed from a place of love and ac-ceptance allows you to reconnect with your more resourceful and powerful self. If you can't do that on your own, do it with a friend who understands the process and knows how amazing you really are.

Assembling your lifeboats means preparing for the eventual certainty that, at some point, you'll need to be saved from yourself. In the context of people lifeboats, that means selecting one or two likely can-didates, friends you think are wise and compassion-ate, and preparing them by explaining in advance what you'll need when you're stressing out. Here's how:

Start by making a request. *"Listen, Jane, I'm try-ing to deal better with the stress in my life, and I've learned a few tools to calm my mind and get back to center. But I'm not that good at it yet. Would you be willing to help me when I'm having trouble help-ing myself?"*

Assuming they agree, you'll want to say some-thing like this: *"Great, thanks. What I'm looking for when I'm in my stuff is for someone who knows me and loves me to just listen without trying to fix the problem or agree with my perspective, but to just smile and remind me that I'm bigger than the way I feel right then. Can you do that for me?"*

If you have one or two friends who can do that, you're fortunate indeed. Between the new attitudes and perspectives you're practicing, the tools in your arsenal to dissolve negative emotions, and the remarkable gift of true friendship, you're in a position to withstand enormous pressure and turn your suffering into enlightenment.

And, of course, you can reciprocate. Practice being that kind of friend yourself. Discipline yourself not to commiserate and agree with your suffering friends about the offenses and resentments they're nursing, but show them who they really are. Listen without fixing; give them the space in your silence to say what they need to say until they've gotten it out of their systems and can start to resonate with your loving view of them. Be that friend, and you'll transform suffering into power.

The second kind of lifeboat is a system lifeboat. Whenever you're off-center, stressed out, or overtaken by negative emotion, you're not at your best. Your decision-making capabilities are limited, and your capacity for virtues like patience and kindness is being stretched to the limit.

If you're drowning in a sea of emotion, you're not in a position to help others or even to choose wisely among your various options.

That's why you need to have systems in place and to have drilled them so thoroughly that they come naturally to you. Like the story I told about instrument flight, you need to be able take systematic, pre-planned action rather than flying by the seat of your pants. In times of high stress, your mastery of systems may be the only thing to save you.

A system can be a single rule, like **LEARN TO SAY NO,** or an entire checklist of action steps for a given situation. The important thing is that the system has value to you and has been thought out in advance.

Here's the problem: **Your ego will always work against your systems.** For example, if you've constructed a checklist of things to do when you're about to snap, and someone tells you that you look like you're about to snap, chances are good that instead of running to your checklist, you'll defend yourself and deny what they're saying. You'll tell them and yourself you're just fine and you can handle whatever is going on. You don't need a freaking checklist!

That's why you need to take your ego out of the equation. Your checklists, whether they be triage rules or business protocols or emergency action steps, must be honored above the way you feel. And if one of your checklists is specifically designed for the times you know you're likely to get stubborn, make item number one on the list an admonition to your ego.

For example, in your wallet or taped to the back of your desk is a list of eight things to do when you're starting to lose it. Maybe items 2-8 are:

- Stop what I'm doing
- Take three deep breaths
- Focus on my sensations, not my thoughts
- Commit to changing my attitude
- Sing "The Greatest Love" to myself
- Drink a glass of water
- Find a funny joke online and have a good laugh

But Item #1 says: **Do this whether I like it or not, if anyone says I've lost my cool!**

Systems work. Checklists work. But only if you use them. And as long as you're relying on your own prodigious mind, you'll resist using them every time. Know that in advance and act accordingly. Forewarned is forearmed!

Necessary strength is a moving target. You've got as much strength as you've developed thus far, and it will continue to grow as you continue to practice. Eventually, you'll be bulletproof, impervious to the aggravations and insults of life being hurled your way. But in the meantime, you'll inevitably find yourself in situations where you don't have necessary strength. And in those times, you need your lifeboats.

Cultivate supportive friendships, draw up checklists that make sense to you, and humble yourself enough to turn to both whenever your stress becomes overwhelming. In fact, if you really want to thrive, don't wait that long!

Important points from Chapter Seven:

- Lifeboats are strategies for surviving when you don't have necessary strength
- People and systems can be lifeboats
- Choose your friends carefully to be lifeboats and train them on what you need
- Develop systems to make your actions automatic for when you lack wisdom
- Prepare in advance for the tendency of your ego to fight you about support

These Exercises For Chapter Seven:

What are your go-to habits when the heat gets too hot? Listening to sad music? Drinking? Smoking? Lashing out? Isolating yourself? Often, your knee jerk habits are detrimental. What you need are pattern interruptions; things that get you out of your old habits and into positive new ones that elevate your mood and make you more resourceful.

Take this week to have fun with these ideas...

• **Compile a list of three friends you consider lifeboats as described in Chapter Seven.** These are reliable individuals who get you but won't placate you, people who can get you back to being you. Make sure they're on speed dial! Let them know you've chosen them for a specific reason, like "I know you won't just tell me I'm right!" Make sure to reciprocate and be there for them when they need a lifeboat.

• **Make a crisis checklist.** What behaviors can you put on automatic that are personal and powerful enough to get you out of your rut. At the top of the list, make a rule for yourself that you'll follow your own advice even if you feel resistance.

Print out both lists. Trim them to fit in a wallet or purse and have them laminated.

• **Check your go-to music selection.** Is it uplifting you or keeping you stuck in an unresourceful place? Years ago a friend confided in me that she was depressed and couldn't figure out why. As I chatted with her, we discovered she was listening to music from the 70s, her most painful time. Without being aware of it, she was reliving the emotions from her teenage years. So take a moment this week to make some new selections, music that will inspire and uplift you.

• Put your new exercises into practice whenever negativity takes hold and you're unable to find the high road. Make a note of how quickly you regained composer, overcame self pity, and got back in the game.

Chapter Eight:
In The Trenches

"If you really want to escape the things that harass you, what you're needing is not to be in a different place but to be a different person."

—Seneca, Letters from a Stoic

Woody is more than my pet; he's my best friend, my buddy, my travel companion, and recently we had to fly to San Diego to speak at a sales meeting for an energy company. We're on a three-leg journey from Burlington. First leg, no problem. Woody even gets his own seat. Second leg's delayed three hours because—get this—they can't find the pilot.

Finally they either find him or train a new one (they certainly had time), and four hours later we're in Dallas. We run outside. Woody does his business. We turn to come back in. Security's closed for the night. We run to the next terminal. Get through security. Run back to our gate, just in time to load up … and sit on the tarmac for two hours. I can only assume the pilot's lost again.

Eventually, they bring us back to the gate. We wait an hour. Back on the plane. Wait an hour. Back to the gate and they cancel the flight. People are going ballistic.

We get off the plane and I try to figure out how I'm going to get us to San Diego in time for my talk tomorrow afternoon and how I'm going to get Woody outside without getting locked out of the airport.

I guess I wasn't planning fast enough, because all of a sudden, Woody lets loose; he pees all over the floor. He's mortified, poor baby, that's not his style. I'm thinking about what to do; comfort him, clean up, get crime scene tape—when suddenly, this very angry-looking woman in a uniform runs up and starts screaming at me.

"Is that your dog?!!"
Obviously.
"He just peed all over the place!!!"
Yes, I see that.
"He can't do that!!!!"
I think he just did. And trust me, he had no choice. We were trapped on the plane for HOURS.
"That doesn't matter! It's NOT allowed!!!"
Now I'm hoping he pees on her.

Anyway, we get that taken care of and end up sleeping (and I use that term loosely) on cots in the middle of the terminal. Woody even gets his own cot for being such a trooper.

The next morning we hop a flight to Orange County, where we rent a car and drive to San Diego, just in time for my talk.

I call that story **Pee Here Now,** and I tell it to you because, in the midst of it all, when those around me were losing their you-know-what, I realized something profound.

I was happy. All my inner work had actually paid off, because I really believed that everything ultimately works out and what's really important is who we're being, moment by moment. I want to live in a world where people take responsibility for who they're being, rather than coming unglued about a urinating dog. What about you?

What would it be like if you were one of the most peaceful, loving, enlightened, and influential people ever to have lived, and you found yourself in the middle of a battlefield? What if you could bring to bear all the elements of the five-step formula we've discussed in the most harried, stressful, intense situations of your life—in such a way that, regardless of the demands of your surroundings, you were at your best and unaffected by the flying bullets?

Let's talk now about the practical application of spiritual principles, the ultimate culmination of the strategies we've explored, and distill them down to a list of ideas to sustain you in the midst of life's greatest challenges. Each of these ideas has its origins in one or more of the five steps, and each has been used to great effect in the trenches, by me and by thousands of others I've coached or taught directly or through my works.

Battlefield Concept #1: Your Work is Your Sadhana

Sadhana is a Sanskrit word meaning daily spiritual practice. Often we do our jobs and live our lives with one set of principles and engage in our spiritual or religious practices with an entirely different set of principles.

We go to church on Sundays but curse the driver who cut us off on the way there. We practice meditation but get anxious if we're late for our yoga class. We try to create a sense of calm in our private time, but we allow ourselves to become agitated when we're performing our daily tasks.

This is a huge contradiction. Spiritual practice is about personal transformation in every area of your life. The purpose of meditation is not to be a meditator, but to be free. The spiritual tools that we use to experience inner peace aren't meant just for the time we're on the cushion. They're meant for the rest of our lives as well, maybe more so. If mindfulness practices don't lead to a change in how we experience our daily lives, they're of no use to us.

Further, we make the mistake of believing that structured practices such as meditation, prayer, and contemplation are the only tools for enlightenment, when in fact they're just training wheels. Once you recognize the reality that everything you do every day is of equal value for your spiritual growth, you begin to appreciate the challenges as if they're the same thing as meditation.

So, you don't need to rush through your aggravating day to get home and sit. You can use whatever is going on right now as a form of meditation. Whereas, in conventional meditative practices, you observe your breath or bodily sensations, notice when your mind wanders, and bring it back to the sensations, in using your work as sadhana, you focus deeply on what you're doing, notice when your mind wanders, and bring it back to the activity.

It's essentially exactly the same thing. In both cases, you're strengthening your focus muscles and becoming aware of where your attention goes. If you're in a high-pressure job, this is even more valuable. You stand a greater chance of releasing your old baggage and connecting with your source energy than others in less difficult circumstances, because you have more opportunities to focus, wander, recognize, and return your awareness to the moment. The more cycles of recognition, the stronger you become.

So, the first battlefield concept is this. Starting tomorrow, go to work grateful that you've been given the gift of sadhana right there in your own job. You don't have to close up shop and move to India to live in an ashram. Your crazy workplace is the perfect laboratory for studying and refining your mind!

Battlefield Concept #2: Never Go Into Battle Without a Battle Plan and a Contingency Plan

I don't know what your job entails, but you do. If you've been there for any length of time, you're aware of what a normal day looks like and what an out-of-control day looks like. You also know what's important and what's not. And you know where and when certain things are likely to occur.

If you've been going into your workplace and feeling surprised or taken aback by the things you don't like, you're just not paying attention. You shouldn't be getting caught off-guard very often, because you know who's kind and who's mean, where things get backed up, when you're most likely to see the most action, and when you're most apt to have downtime.

If you were treating your job with the impeccability we discussed in Chapter Four, you'd be studying the patterns of your job and making a "battle plan" based on what you know. This could even be a group effort. You sit down with your colleagues and list the things that create stress. Maybe there's an area where a lot happens, and the clutter there is diminishing effectiveness. Maybe John doesn't like the music Andrea plays in her cubicle. Maybe there's a specific kind of a person who shows up in your workplace that Eleanor is very comfortable dealing with, but whom Art finds intimidating. Maybe there are times when twelve things are happening all at once and nobody really knows which should be handled first.

Once you've begun that process, you can create specific action steps to cover each eventuality. You can create a protocol for dealing with potentially overwhelming situations, you can make agreements about how people should communicate with one another, and you can set aside specific blocks of time to work "on the business" rather than "in the business."

And, you can have contingency plans. What do we do when something unexpected happens? Do we meet and discuss it? Do we turn the decision over to Barbara? Do we duck into the break room and down a fifth of Jack Daniels? What's the strategy?

The better you plan for the expected and even unexpected stressors of your job, the more you can stay on track without losing valuable time or mental resources trying to invent a strategy on the fly.

Commit yourself tomorrow to scheduling a planning session to create agreement about the stressors of your job, and then plan at least one follow-up session, during which you can evaluate and refine the battle plan you've made.

Battlefield Concept #3: Philosophical Assessment

Let's say you're playing a game of tennis. The ball crosses the net on its way to you. You size it up. You wait for the right moment. And you swing. Let's say you miss. In that moment, one of two things will happen.

You might participate in what's called "psychological assessment." That's when your mind gets busy giving you all the feedback you don't really want or need. I can't believe I missed that shot! That's the third time I let the ball slip right past my forehand! I should give this game up and take up volleyball instead! Why did I ever think I'd be able to play tennis???

Meanwhile, the game has proceeded on, and you're spiraling deeper and deeper into mediocrity. Your noisy mind is ruining your moment, and while it's busy criticizing your immediate past, it's simultaneously ensuring disappointment in your immediate future.

The other thing you might do instead is called "philosophical assessment." In that scenario, you swing, miss, and your mind says, "Next!" And then, it shuts up.

Your capacity to handle things coming at you quickly, whether they be tennis balls or customer complaints, is directly proportional to the degree of silence in your head. Although we don't like to accept it, the reality is that our cerebral cortex, the thinking part of our minds, isn't nearly as agile as our cerebellum and brainstem, which coordinate our movements and immediate responses to environmental change.

Great athletes, like the samurai of old, understand that there's something called body knowing. Your body will respond to attack much more quickly than your thinking mind. If you've been properly trained, that response will be immediate, innate, and appropriate. If, on the other hand, you think about how you should react, by the time the thought has registered in your brain, it's too late.

In the movie The Last Samurai, Tom Cruise's mentor, a great samurai warrior, watches him train and comments on his swordsmanship by yelling, "Too much mind! No mind! No mind!" He's admonishing his student to quiet his mind.

Think of this the next time you're on the battlefield of your job. More than anything else, you must quiet your mind and trust your training. If you're upset, your mind is not quiet. You can't be upset and quiet at the same time.

So, the next time something troubling happens at work or you find yourself criticizing your own past performance, try screaming to yourself: Next!

Battlefield Concept #4: Take a beat, not a beating

As you develop greater mastery over your mind through mindfulness training, you'll notice that things don't come at you quite as fast. But in the meantime, the slings and arrows that are flying around your head are moving much more rapidly than you can parry them.

The problem is, once you miss the first one, not only are you less prepared for the next one, but you're fairly likely to add to the problem by shooting one or two at yourself. Buddhists call that "the second arrow."

First, you get shot, metaphorically speaking. Maybe someone insults you or lashes out at you. Then, you shoot yourself by attacking how you let yourself be shot. What's the matter with me! I let him walk right up to me and disrespect me! I suck! Hopefully, you see the poignant humor of that.

So, stress under normal circumstances means a combination of external attacks and internal attacks against yourself for having succumbed to the external attacks. Really, it's funny.

Instead, build in pauses throughout your day. They needn't last long. But the moment you're at a crossroads and don't know how to proceed, give yourself the space of a breath or two to figure out the most positive choice you can make. The more you can create a beat between stimulus and response, the more informed will be your response.

Again, it doesn't have to be long ... but it should be deep. Learn to get as quiet inside as you can, as quickly as you can, and take a beat so as to give every stimulus a chance to be evaluated by your wiser self before you react automatically or emotionally.

Battlefield Concept #5: Triage

If you're in a medical field, this concept is not new to you. When a tragedy has occurred and the waiting room is filling with victims, you need to make rapid decisions about who to help first, who can wait, and who is beyond your help. Every business has some form of protocol. There's always either a preordained or self-evident order in which things should be done. There are things of high value and urgency that must be done first. There are others that might be equally important but less urgent, so they can wait until second. There are perhaps goals you've set that, in light of current circumstances, are no longer viable, and these can be dismissed.

The mistake many make in the heat of the moment is to ignore the protocols and try to do everything at once. This is a doomed plan. We like to believe we're capable of multitasking, but study after study proves that we're much more productive and far less stressed when we size up the work before us, prioritize it, and take it on piece by piece in the correct order. Treat your job as if it were an emergency situation, and triage your "patients."

Battlefield Concept #6: Powerbreak

Unfortunately, in the throes of a high-pressure day, sometimes a beat isn't enough, but a full-blown meditation session is too much. What do you do when you've only got a couple of minutes and need to replenish yourself? Here's a technique I synthesized from a few different disciplines. It's a powerful way to recharge your mental and emotional battery in a relatively short period of time.

It's helpful whenever you're under stress or feeling overwhelmed, or if your energy level, mood, confidence, or presence fall below healthy levels. You can build Powerbreaks into your daily schedule as preventive care for your mind and body.

People who perform a Powerbreak every couple of

hours maintain a higher level of energy and productivity, and complete their days with greater optimism and humor.

A Powerbreak is meant to be done in three-minute increments, as follows ...

1. Sit quietly in a place where you'll be left alone. Close your eyes. Take three deep breaths. With every breath in, picture yourself breathing in relaxation. With every exhalation, picture yourself releasing stress and tension.
2. With the middle finger of your right hand, tap on the area in the middle of your forehead just above your eyebrows for ten repetitions.
3. Place your hands comfortably in your lap and put your attention on that same area. As you continue to breathe slowly, deeply, and evenly, imagine that your breath is coming in and out through that spot.*
4. If you're experiencing any negative emotions or unwanted thoughts, say to yourself: I release this feeling. I release this thought. Again, return to the area on your forehead.
5. Now, repeat the following affirmation silently for five repetitions, contemplating its meaning for you: Every day in every way, I'm getting better and better. **
6. End your session with three more deep breaths and open your eyes.
7. Notice how this brief Powerbreak quickly recharges you and prepares you for your next challenge!

*You may see flashes of light or feel a glowing feeling. You may notice your eyes beginning to flutter. You may also notice tingling in various parts of your body. Whatever you feel is OK. Just observe it and try to keep your attention on that area.

**This is a 100-year-old affirmation coined by Emile Coue, the father of Autosuggestion.

Battlefield Concept #7: Premature closure

Yesterday I was walking Woody on the bike path and thinking about home, which is where we were headed. I felt myself speeding up, anxious to get home. The increased pace was not only uncomfortable, but also unsatisfying. Somehow I had an unformed idea that I should be home now, and there was no way I could walk fast enough to be there that quick. Interestingly, I didn't really have any reason to get home, anyway. It was just a feeling.

When I noticed it, I thought about how often we seek premature closure. We have a problem. We want it solved now. We know that there are steps to take and that time must pass, but we harbor an inner feeling of discontent that pushes us onward at a pace faster than is comfortable, yet slower than is satisfying.

I was reminded of an earlier time when I was stuck in traffic and started to notice a subtle yet distinct scootching of my body forward in the car seat, as if I could push the entire line of stopped traffic forward with my powerful butt. Once I noticed it, I laughed, but it wasn't long before I caught myself doing it again—subconsciously trying to move things forward energetically rather than accepting where I was and relaxing.

When we get into that mindset, we're forever agitated. We want what we can't have: for the thing to be over. And we go into a tizzy of activity to try to be done with the thing—to no avail.

Wanting it over, wanting premature closure, is a trap. It's a way for our busy minds to keep us stuck in the future rather than accepting the present. It makes us uneasy with ourselves, less effective, and addicted to fruitless effort.

When you find yourself literally or energetically trying to scootch forward faster than you can in an effort to get somewhere now, when in fact that can't be done, notice the pattern and stop it right away. Immediately tell yourself that where you are is OK and that, step by step, you'll arrive at the point of closure exactly when you're supposed to.

We used to say "you can't push the river," and that's exactly what this process does; it reminds you that all things come to fruition in their own time.

Battlefield Concept #8: Strategic mindfulness

We've said that mindfulness is a state of heightened awareness with a quality of non-judgmental acceptance; it's a state in which you're awake and conscious of where your energy and attention is being directed.

But of course, there are infinite places your energy could be directed. You might be thinking about a problem or its solution, the past or the future, an unpleasant or pleasant thought, your body, your breath, or any number of things.

And it's possible to do all of them mindfully. You can mindfully focus on the past. You can mindfully focus on the present. The difference between mindful focus and being "lost in thought" is your awareness of the fact that you're doing it. You're not lost. You've just chosen to direct your energy somewhere.

There are times when you'd be better off immersing yourself in the vision of your new future...

In terms of the choices and decisions you must make under pressure or the goals you must set to create a better future than your current circumstance, there are times when it's appropriate to daydream. There are times when you'd be far better off immersing yourself in the vision of your new future than ruminating about your unsatisfying present. And there are other times when you should be right here, right now, dealing with what's right in front of you.

When you choose to direct your mind to the future, do so either for proactive planning purposes (like buying insurance) or to create a pleasant picture of what could be. Don't allow yourself to direct your mind to worry. Worry is a misuse of the powers of visualization and can only be done without mindfulness. So, being strategic in your mindfulness means deciding when to focus on the present, when to focus on the future, and how to use your vision of what is yet to be in a way that helps you attain it—by seeing a pleasant image toward which you can move. Seldom is it valuable to focus on the past, but even that could have its value.

But regardless of where you direct your attention, do so consciously and in a way that produces positive value. Be strategic in your use of mindfulness.

Battlefield Concept #9: Spot, Stop, Dissolve, Replace

Picture this. You're walking along eating a hot pastrami sandwich on rye with deli mustard, not paying much attention. Without your noticing it, a big glob of mustard oozes out of the back end of the sandwich and lands on your nice white shirt. You walk by a closed shop, and the darkened window reflects your image back to you. You spot the spot.

The next thing you do is you stop eating the sandwich. You were almost done anyway, and you're right around the corner from home. So you drop it into the nearest trash can, run home, remove the shirt, and dab the stain with some OxiClean to dissolve it as quickly as possible.

You wash the shirt, your only good white shirt, and put it back on since you have an important meeting later. On the way out, you realize you're still hungry. But you don't want to make the same mistake as before, so you grab an apple instead of something that will stain your shirt.

What you've done is to **SPOT** the spot, **STOP** the activity that caused it, **DISSOLVE** the spot, and **REPLACE** the offending substance with something safer (and better for you).

OK, let's take that idea into the battlefield of life. The formula—the only thing you need to remember out here, since it's cumbersome to try to carry a whole book's worth of transformational technology with you—consists of four words: **SPOT, STOP, DISSOLVE, REPLACE.**

Let's try it.

It's been a tough day so far. Three people have yelled at you, your administrative assistant has made a couple of big mistakes, and you have to let someone go. You're stressing out and don't even realize it.

Your wife calls and asks you to pick up the kids from school—and you snap. One damn thing too many! You hang up after a tense interaction, not feeling very good about it.

Suddenly, you **SPOT** the stress you're feeling, exemplified and made clear by what a jerk you just were.

If you're wise, you'll now **STOP** doing whatever is causing you all that stress—maybe close your office door and shut out the world for a few minutes.

Now, you could call your wife back or you could sit there and beat yourself up, but if you're wise, you'll first turn your attention away from the incident, away from the irritating things that happened today, and away from any self-abuse, and you'll simply observe the tense sensations in your body, knowing that to do so without mental rumination will cause them to **DISSOLVE.**

Once they've dissolved and you're back to center, you can **REPLACE** them with a whole new attitude. Maybe you can make a gratitude list. Maybe you could go sit with your admin and see how you could help her do her job better. Maybe you could watch a funny video and replace your lousy mood with a happy one. (And then, you'd better pick up flowers on the way home for your wife!)

But regardless of which actions you choose, each of them is going to be executed with the intention of honoring **SPOT, STOP, DISSOLVE,** and **REPLACE.**

That's a quick, in-the-trenches way of regaining your center and finding peace.

Battlefield Concept #10: Bless this mess

I call this last battlefield concept **bless this mess.**
Non-acceptance is your real enemy, much more so
than the situation you find yourself in. Whenever you
refuse to accept what is, whenever you rail against the
now, you lose.

That's not to say that you should roll over and play
dead. It means that what is, is. It may not be what you're
shooting for, and you're welcome to try to change it, but
for the moment, this is your reality. **Don't reject it mentally.**
Don't churn about how it shouldn't be.

It's been said that whenever you and reality come into
conflict, reality always wins. Stop resisting what is. What
you resist persists. You're much more likely to change
things when you start from an acceptance that they are
the way they are than if you start with anger, resentment,
and disbelief.

One of the most powerful ways to rapidly open to the
now is by blessing it. Just accept the idea that there's
something hidden in the moment that is inherently good,
and imagine yourself sending it the energy of gratitude
and love, regardless of the outward appearance of the
situation.

While this may sound a little New Agey or woo-woo, let
me be clear. I'm not suggesting you have any magical
powers or spiritual gifts to change the situation. Nor am I
suggesting that you're a faith healer. What I am suggesting is that the intention to meet the situation with love
and gratitude transforms you as a person. It relieves you
of the stress of fighting what is. And, it just feels good.

Use your imagination, your powers of visualization, to
create an image of yourself connected by beams of light
to the stressful situation. What you'll find, as thousands
have, is that your imagination will lead you to a more relaxed state in which you're embracing rather than resisting your high-pressure situation.

So, there are ten quick, in-the-trenches methods of
reducing your stress and increasing your effectiveness. By
using your mind in a deliberate and focused way, wheth-

er through imagination or reframing your thinking, you'll gain mastery over your emotions and find peace in the midst of your most stressful moments. You can truly be bulletproof in the trenches!

Important points from Chapter Eight:

- It's more important who you're being than what you're doing
- Your daily work can be your daily spiritual practice
- Create a clear battle plan to minimize your stress
- Master a couple of ways to quiet your mind for different lengths of time
- Prioritize your objectives by importance and urgency
- Use the **SPOT, STOP, DISSOLVE, REPLACE** method

Chapter Nine:
Your Bulletproof Life

"The cave you fear to enter holds the treasure you seek."
—Joseph Campbell

*"Our job is unconditional love. The job of everyone else
in our life is to push our buttons."*

—Byron Katie

Let me take you on a journey into the future. It's been
a little over a year since you read this book. You're looking back over the past twelve months and appreciating
the transformation you've undergone and all the ways
you've benefited from what you've learned. Comparing
your old life to your new one is very satisfying and almost
unbelievable.

You realize you used to think of stress as something
real. In fact, you were dead certain that the only way to

overcome stress was to get out of the crazy situation you were in. As far as you knew, stress came from outside of you. High-pressure situations were stressful by their nature, and the degree of stress was directly proportional to the intensity of the pressure.

But now you see stress in an entirely new way. Your stress is proportional not to external pressure but to the amount of negative mental activity you give it. You understand that nothing outside of you is guaranteed to cause you stress. You realize that different people experience the same pressure in different ways. And you've chosen to be one of those people who, rather than resisting the pressure of your job, relishes it. To you, it's become a dance. The pressure arises, you welcome it, and you find the most creative way of moving with it to produce satisfying outcomes and to experience a wonderful sense of accomplishment.

Your stress is proportional not to external pressure but to the amount of negative mental activity you give it.

You often think back to Superman, bullets flying toward him and bouncing off as he smiles a confident smile. You now see how you're doing the same thing. Whether you're facing high-stakes presentations, hirings, firings, mergers, or sensitive conversations with co-workers, you now recognize that the metaphoric bullets flying your way have no power to destroy you, and that makes you feel very happy.

You're beginning to take back your power. You understand that you control your own thoughts and feelings. You've come to realize that between every stimulus and every response is a moment, a beat, during which you get to make mindful choices about how you'll react to that stimulus.

You also realize that your ability to take that beat is directly proportional to your inner strength, so you've willingly embraced the inner work that develops that strength. You've been meditating and doing other mindfulness practices, and as a result, you can feel yourself becoming noticeably calmer, happier, and wiser.

You've also let go of the arrogance you used to have

when you thought you could handle it all by yourself. You've developed systems to fall back on, and you've invited friends into your life with whom you're comfortable revealing your emotional challenges.

You're beginning to love the kind of support you've learned to give and receive. Instead of the old way, where you'd say you felt bad and somebody would tell you not to feel that way, you now see the value of being witnessed in silence. You can tell your friends all your frustrations and they listen with love in their hearts until you eventually talk yourself through your frustration and out the other side to your wisdom.

As you've learned to witness yourself and be witnessed by others, you can see the changeable nature of the things you once thought were unchangeable. You used to think a frustrating situation was just that, by definition. **But now, after many experiences of working through your feelings, you can see that your attitude can shift, and with it, the situation itself.** The exact same situation has a completely different quality, and new choices appear when your attitude changes.

You now understand the Seneca quote about how you don't need to change your circumstances but to change yourself. And now, you know how.

You also think back to the amphipod, that foot-long shrimp-like creature living below seven miles of ocean, thriving under the most intense pressure on Earth. And you recognize yourself as a human amphipod. The pressure hasn't left, but now you're thriving.

You can see how the dance of thriving under pressure has two primary steps. **One is the adoption of a new attitude,** one not victimized by stress. The other is the **adoption of intelligent strategies** to minimize confusion, inefficiency, and conflict.

And since it's a dance, you realize that it's all about moving seamlessly between the two, each supporting the other. So, you step toward greater relaxation in the midst of pressure, which then allows you to bring your wisdom to your current situation and find better ways to do things. And that, in turn, helps you relax even more, which again leads you to better problem solving ... and the dance goes on!

You are becoming bulletproof.

Amid the pressure, the challenges, the conflicts and the crises, you know how to maintain your serenity and your wisdom. You know this is working, because you've caught yourself more than a few times smiling in the middle of a tense moment. You've had several sudden recognitions that, despite all the frustrating things happening around you, you weren't frustrated. And in all the high-stakes situations where everyone around you was freaking out, you kept your cool.

People are beginning to notice this shift in you. You're calmer, happier, wiser, and more fun to be around. You joke at times when in the past you would have frozen up or taken things way too seriously. Your new attitude is having an impact on your job prospects. More people value your contribution, which might mean more sales, upward mobility in your company, leadership opportunities, or just the chance to be around more influential people.

And recently, you've even begun to notice people coming to you for advice and counsel. They gravitate toward you because you calm them and give them hope. It seems as if your wise, untroubled nature is contagious. Some around you are beginning to show signs of being the same way. Others are curious and want to know how they can be more like you. And you're happy to share your journey with them.

You tell them about meditation and powerbreaks and taking a beat and other tools you've learned to use and master. You're loving that you're a source of wisdom for others, and you're hopeful that you'll soon see a shift in your company's culture as more people embrace these powerful ideas. You're a pebble in the pond, and the ripples go out indefinitely.

One of the most amazing things that's happened in the past several months is that you've made friends with some of your prior adversaries. **First, you befriended your situation, so you were no longer at odds with the reality of your work.** Then, you started meeting those who used to challenge you emotionally with compassion and humor rather than hostility and fear. You actually feel something welling up inside you when you think about those shifts—how you've watched the most irritating, obnoxious, hostile people turn into cherished colleagues with the underlying goodness that you've found in them. You realize you've witnessed magic.

You're aware of how each of the five steps in the Bulletproof formula have changed you.

First, you acknowledged the goal of happiness. Second, **you committed to cleaning up your act:** bringing discipline, order, and morality to your actions. Third, **you began to practice focus,** disciplining yourself to keep your attention on a specific point of concentration for long periods of time. Fourth, **you began to see the dawn of wisdom** as you began to embrace rather than fight reality. And fifth, you developed a network of support to help you through those challenges for which you weren't yet ready.

You've become less attached to outcomes, more accepting of what is, more lighthearted in your approach to goals, and more reverent about your own underlying goodness and that of those around you. Nothing is permanent, and nothing requires your suffering.

Looking back at this very transformative year, you can be grateful that you've discovered these principles and had the courage and tenacity to stick with the practices that have made them real in every area of your life. And you can hardly wait to see what's next!

OK, let's return to the present moment. The journey we've just taken is a process called future pacing. It's a powerful process designed to help you envision a desired outcome and move towards it.

More powerful than having me create your future story is for you to do it. So, my recommendation is that you take an hour and write your own version of this story.

The process is simple. Write about how your life has changed for the better, being as specific as you can about what your new life looks like, feels like, and sounds like. What are you thinking? What emotions are you feeling? What are you now able to do that you couldn't do before? How do you feel about that? What impact are you now making on the world? Where will you go from here?

As you write, do so in the first person and present tense. In other words, don't write *"I will ..." but "I am ..."* See yourself already in the future you desire, and write from that place. Also, avoid negatives. Instead of "I'm not anxious and neurotic," write, *"I am now confident and fearless ..."*

This future pacing exercise will be greatly valuable for you if you take the time to do it. You'll probably feel a sense of excitement and hopefulness as you write, and you're also likely to discover a few surprises along the way—wants that you've repressed, perhaps because you never thought they were possible, but which now spill out onto the page as you fantasize your perfect future.

Finally, as you do this exercise, reflect on the specific lessons of this book. Use the tools and techniques in your narrative so you're able to say that you are now medi-tating, doing the SPOT/STOP technique, or any other of the many tools provided here. In that way, you'll increase your chances of actually using them, since they're part of your future story.

Again, make it a priority to review your goals and dreams, lessons and revelations, and know that living amid stress and pressure is within your capability.

This is just the beginning!

Chapter 10:
Conclusion and Challenge

We've come at last to the end of this road together. But it's only the beginning of yours.

In these pages, I've shared powerful secrets of serenity and wisdom; performance and productivity. Each of the tools, techniques, and perspectives I've shared have been proven to work in amazing and surprising ways. Some of the material is directly taken from ancient works of spiritual and philosophical wisdom. Some is drawn from the recent surge of interest from the scientific community in the nature of the mind. Brain research has gone very far in validating ancient truths about things like happiness, mindfulness, and compassion.

It's my personal desire that you use the ideas here to transform your life and to make a difference in the lives of others. This can only be done if you take the ideas off the page and bring them into your life.

With that in mind, I'm going to issue you a challenge. Every chapter of this book contains multiple ideas about how to fulfill the intentions of the specific step outlined in that chapter.

For example, in the chapter on happiness, you got a baker's dozen techniques proven to elevate happiness. When we discussed cleaning up your act, there was another list of practical ideas to become more organized and to live with a higher level of integrity. In the next part, we drilled down deeply into several ways of increasing your focus. The fourth step was all about leaning in to your pain and pressure, and I gave you some practical tips to do that. The fifth step in the process was about creating a support system for yourself, and we discussed showing friends how they can best support you and developing systems to keep you on track in the face of emotional upheaval.

I even gave you a chapter about how to use the many concepts "on the battlefield" of your life. That chapter contained shortcuts for those times that you feel under fire. Knowing that it's difficult to draw on a large body of knowledge when times are tense, I tried to give you practical applications that would embody the teachings without requiring you to open up the entire file cabinet of your mind.

And the last chapter was about seeing yourself as having already transformed your life, creating an image toward which you could strive.

Here's the challenge: Take at least one idea from each chapter and give it a try for three weeks. Put your heart and soul into it, and don't prejudge the outcome. Stay humble. Remember that your ego will always try to convince you that what you're thinking, or what you think you know, is right—an irrefutable fact.

Hopefully, by now you know otherwise. Your ego will lead you down all sorts of blind alleys, pompously championing its own worldview.

You are more than your ego. You are more than your mind. You are more than your thoughts. You can be bulletproof. You can be an amphipod. You can be a monk in the trenches. All you need to do is start with humility, surrendering to the reality that, left to your own devices, you'll default to a lesser version of yourself; and then decide that you're ready to live a happy, stress-free life. From there, it's just a matter of doing the work. Stay the course, trust the process, be patient, resist the urge to run or slack off, and remind yourself of the benefit of doing that.

There's nothing I've written here that I haven't used myself to great benefit. My early days of neurosis, anxiety, and depression were the impetus for my exhaustive study of the mind, and my only interest at the beginning of this process was to end my suffering. I feel that I've done that. I have a new relationship with pain and stress, and I feel a measure of freedom, even in the face of difficult times.

As I've learned to make these principles part of my life, I've simultaneously felt moved to share them with others. So, besides my personal experience of success with the tools in this book, I know there are thousands of people who have used my teachings to end their suffering and improve their lots in life.

While I know the power on these pages, I'm also aware of the tendency we all have to read ideas, think they're great, and then do nothing with them. As Joe Charbonneau said, *"Knowledge without implementation leads to depression."*

You have a lot to give, both to your work and to the world. Find your center, become the wise soul you're meant to be, and express your unique gifts. Let the words you've read here live, not on the shelf, but in your life.

I wish you the very best of success and invite you to share your personal stories with me as you embark on your great adventure.

Highly Recommended Reading & Viewing

Books

7 Habits of Highly Effective People
by Stephen Covey

The Art of Living
by William Hart

The Art of Living Consciously
by Nathaniel Branden

Awakening the Giant Within
by Anthony Robbins

Be Here Now by Ram Dass

Cutting Through Spiritual Materialism
by Trungpa Rinpoche

Goals by Brian Tracy

The Greatest Secret in the World
by Og Mandino

Handbook to Higher Consciousness
by Ken Keyes

Invitation to a Great Experiment
by Thomas Powers

The Journey of Awakening
by Ram Dass

Living Buddha, Living Christ by Thich Nat
Han *Meditation Now* by SN Goenka

The Mood Cure by Julia Ross

The One-Minute Millionaire
by Mark Victor Hansen

The Power of Intention by Wayne Dyer

The Power of Now by Eckart Tolle

Power vs. Force by David Hawkins

Prosperity by Charles Fillmore

The Sermon on the Mount by Emmett Fox

Spiritual Economics by Eric Butterworth

Steppenwolf by Herman Hesse

The Teachings of Don Juan
by Carlos Castaneda

Waking Up by Charles Tart

Walden by Henry David Thoreau

The Way of The Peaceful Warrior by Dan Millman

The Sacred Journey of The Peaceful Warrior
by Dan Millman

We're All Doing Time by Bo Lozoff

What the Buddha Taught by Walpola Rahula

Where Are You Going by Swami Muktananda

Movies

The Peaceful Warrior

Based on real events captured in his book The Way of The Peaceful Warrior, Dan Milman (played by Scott Mechlowicz) is a gifted gymnast whose desire to succeed drives everything he does. After a crippling motocycle accident, Dan meets a mysterious stranger (Nick Nolte), who opens Dan's eyes to a new reality.

Field of Dreams

An Iowa farmer (played by Kevin Costner), hears a mysterious voice one night whispering *"If you build it, they will come."* Despite the ridicule of friends and family, he builds a baseball diamond in the middle of his cornfield, complete with lights and bleachers. Once the baseball field is finished, the ghosts of great players start emerging from the field to play ball.

The Shawshank Redemption

Former banker Andy Dufresne (Tim Robbins), falsely accused of murdering his wife and her lover, is sentenced to two consecutive life terms in the maximum security Shawshank State Penitentiary. Andy adjusts to harsh prison life inside the walls of the prison, and forms a friendship with Red (Morgan Freeman). It becomes clear that Andy doesn't belong there, and despite potential evidence that could set him free, the warden does everything possible to keep Andy there for life.

Sentence Stems

The following exercises are based on the work of Nathaniel Branden, psychologist and author of several pivotal works. Dr. Branden recommends sentence completion as a method for becoming more conscious of the workings of your mind. Like me, he advocates conscious awareness or witnessing rather than deliberate efforts at change. He and I feel that the mere act of bringing consciousness to your attitudes, beliefs, and choices unleashes a deep inner process of transformation, and the changes necessary for your personal growth unfold of their own accord. To use these exercises, you'll need a journal, computer, or notebook. Write each sentence stem at the top of a page, and then see how many endings for that sentence you can write in the period of one minute. Do not think about your answers in advance. Just write quickly and as Dr. Branden says, "*Allow your answers to surprise you.*"

I designed these sentence stems to compliment the concepts elucidated in this book. I recommend that you take one day for each grouping of sentence stems and do that whole group twice that day; evaluate and explore your answers at a later time. There are seven groupings with which to work, so you can complete this part of the program in a week. If you complete the entire series of stems, you will discover important information about your attitudes and beliefs, and will be well on your way to transforming your consciousness. Upon completion, I encourage you to start right in with the goal-setting strategies we've discussed. Don't delay your dreams any longer! I wish you great success!

Day 1: "One thing I like about myself is_____" "One thing I don't like about myself is_____" "One of the ways I've limited my success is_____" "When I succeed at something I feel_____" "When I contemplate taking a risk to accomplish something new, I feel_____" "One thing I definitely want in my life is_____"

Day 2

"I feel happiest when I_____" "One thing I'd do even if I weren't getting paid is_____" "Something that I'm proud of about myself is_____" "Lots of people say that I'm_____" "One of the qualities of people I respect is_____" "One way that I lack congruence is_____"

Day 3

"I feel most present when I_____" "I feel least present when I_____" " "One thing I'd do if I knew I couldn't fail is_____" "One thing I believe about myself is_____" "One thing I believe about success is_____" "One thing I believe about successful people is_____"

Day 4

"One recurrent emotion I feel is_____" "One feeling that gets in the way of my success is_____" "When people compliment me I_____" "When people criticize me I_____" "If I could change one thing about my-self_____" "One thing I judge in others is_____"

Day 5

"In my business life, I intend to_____" "In my per-sonal life, I intend to_____" "In my spiritual life, I intend to_____" "Regarding my health, I intend to_____" "Regarding my finances, I intend to_____" "Regarding my relationships, I intend to_____"

Day 6

"If I took complete responsibility for my feelings_____"
"If I took complete responsibility for my success_____" "If I were completely reliable_____" "If I were completely trustworthy_____" "If I had control over my emotions_____"

Day 7

"One thing about me I'm afraid to share is_____"
"One thing I could do to be a better listener is_____" "I could be kinder to_____" "One thing that stops me from asking for help is_____" "The most important thing I've learned about myself is_____" "The first thing I'm going to do to create my life is_____"

An Invitation...

If you've benefited from this book or you would like to share your experience, I'd like to hear from you. Please feel free to write me at steve@stevetaubman.com.
I promise to write back.

About The Author

Dr. Steve Taubman has dedicated his life to showing people how to thrive
through their challenges.
He's written extensively on
the application of contem-
plative practices in stressful
situations and has spoken
throughout the United
States on mindset mastery
for goal-oriented profes-
sionals.

Having endured crippling
anxiety and low self esteem
early in life, Dr. Taubman made it his mission to understand the nature of happiness and the remedy
for emotional turmoil. His search led him to neurolo-
gy, holistic health, mindfulness, positive psychology,
and hypnosis. Each of these disciplines is represent-
ed in Dr. Taubman's system for living a balanced
life, free of neurosis and rich in accomplishment.

Dr. Taubman continues to enrich his understanding of the science of happiness and its impact on
success. Most recently, he's partnered with mental
toughness expert, Steve Siebold, to deliver high impact programs on the psychology of performance

to business professionals worldwide.

When not writing or speaking, Dr. Taubman enjoys spending time with his dog, Woody, in and around his home on the beautiful Burlington, Vermont waterfront.

Did you enjoy your reading of Bulletproof?
Would you like to share the experience? Who do you know that needs the message of this book? Let us help you help them!

Bulletproof makes an excellent birthday or holiday present for a friend or family member in a high pressure job. Give the gift of wisdom and serenity. Order copies at Amazon.com.

For orders of 50 copies or more, contact us directly at: steve@stevetaubman.com.

Made in USA - Kendallville, IN
1070552_9780976627111
12.29.2020 2033